The South African garden

Month by Month

Zoë Gilbert

cna

Author's acknowledgements

My thanks and appreciation to the publishers, and especially to Sandy Warren, for their co-operation in the preparation of this book, and to the Capetonian for his valuable guidance on gardening in the winter rainfall region.

Central News Agency (Pty) Ltd
CNA Building, Laub Street,
New Centre, Johannesburg 2001

First published 1984
Second impression 1985
Third impression 1987
Fourth impression 1988
Fifth impression 1989
Sixth impression 1991

Edited by Sandy Warren
Illustrated by Gina Daniel
Photoset by McManus Bros (Pty) Ltd, Cape Town
Printing and binding by Tien Wah Press Pte Ltd, Singapore

ISBN 0 620 07436 1

Contents

Introduction

Gardening is always a challenge no matter where one lives, but perhaps gardening in South Africa provides an even greater challenge than in most other countries. Our climate varies from sub-tropical to temperate, while in some parts of the country snow is quite common in winter. The Western Cape has a Mediterranean climate, with winter rain, while the interior of the country gets its rain only in summer. There are mist belts, as well as semi-deserts, with many micro-climates in between. One can actually find different micro-climates in one's own garden, and in different parts of the same suburb. The micro-climate found on one side of a range of hills can be quite different to that found on the other side of the range. The micro-climate can differ from the crest of a hill to the valley, or be influenced by prevailing hot or cold winds. Latitude is another factor. Capetonians, for example, being situated further south, usually sow later than gardeners in the north.

This book offers month by month guidance for the gardener. This guidance is based on the conditions that usually prevail in the different parts of the country at a particular time of year. Nature, however, has a mind of her own. Unseasonable weather does occur, and so it is important that gardeners also always follow their own good sense. For example, although March with its cooler weather is usually a good time to start planting bulbs, if your area is right in the middle of a heat wave in March it would obviously be wiser to delay planting until the weather has cooled down.

It also pays to be observant. When moving to a new locality observe what plants are thriving there, and do not be afraid to ask advice from local gardeners as their experience can be most valuable.

Watering is an important aspect of gardening in this country, and *when to water* and *how to water* need to be considered. In winter, water in the morning in cold, frosty areas. This gives the foliage time to dry, and the soil time to warm up again, before nightfall. In summer, water in the late afternoon, except when the humidity is high. The water then has time to seep down into the soil before being evaporated by the hot sun and wind. Lawns, however, should be watered in the morning as fungi are far more likely to attack wet grass at night during hot, humid weather.

Always water thoroughly. A good soaking once or twice a week is infinitely better than a light sprinkling every day. When the soil is wet to a good depth, roots are encouraged to go down deeper in search of moisture. If only the top few centimetres of soil are moistened the roots will stay near the surface, and as soon as the surface of the soil dries out the plants will suffer. The ideal is to keep the soil evenly damp to a good depth, without it being saturated. Plants dislike 'wet feet' and actually 'drown' in waterlogged soil as their roots must breathe.

The more well-made compost that is dug into the soil and used for mulching, the better your plants will grow. Compost improves the structure and water retention of the soil, as well as providing food for the teeming millions of micro-organisms which make the nutrients in the soil available to plants. Mulching helps to conserve moisture and regulate soil temperature, and a layer of mulch keeps the soil cool in summer and warm in winter.

Keep spraying to a minimum. Gardeners can prevent pests from becoming a real problem merely by being observant and dealing with pests as soon as they make an appearance. A

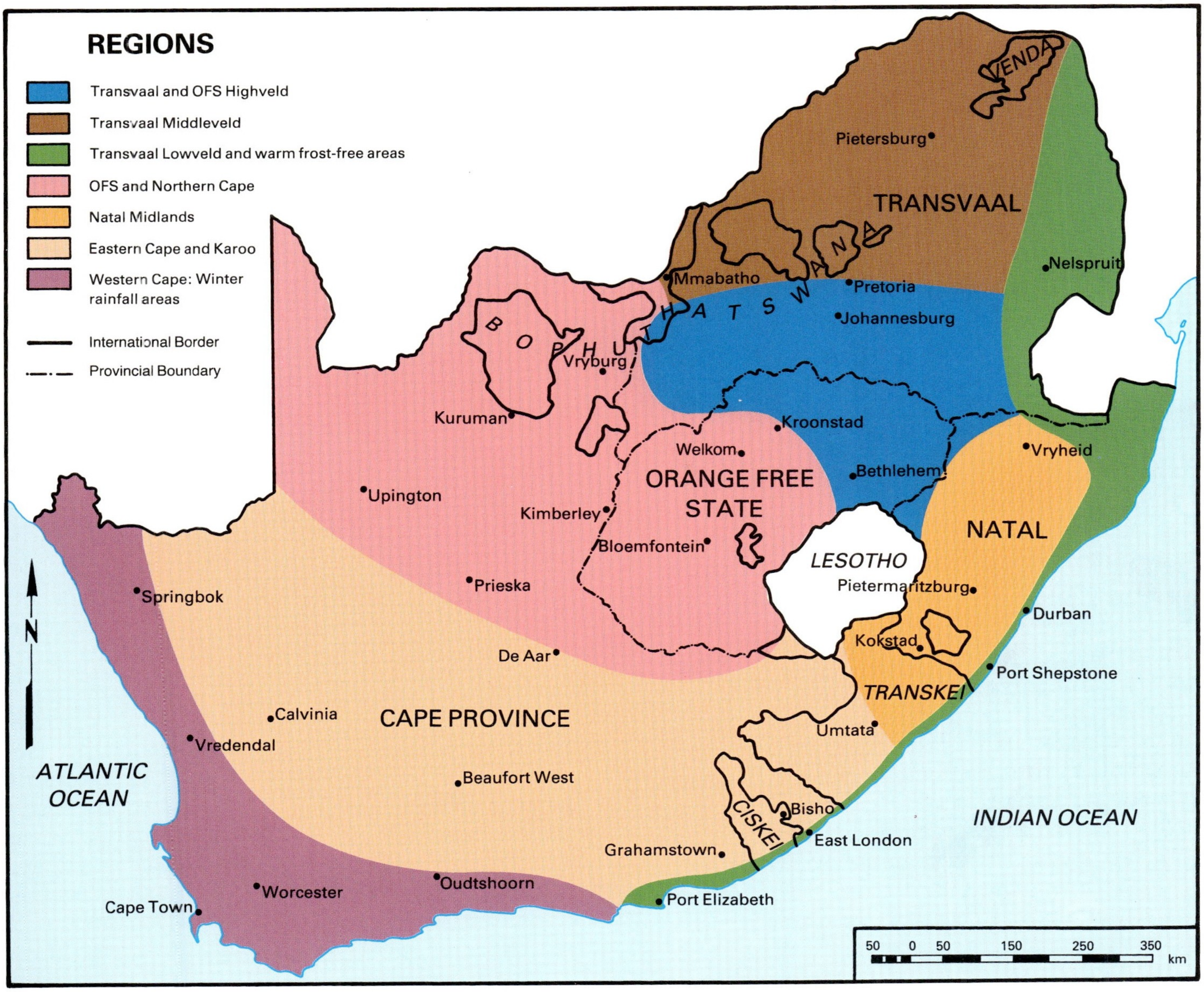

certain amount of preventive spraying must be done, for example, against black spot, rust and mildew on roses, and against fruit fly and codling moth in fruit. The most common garden pests and diseases are fully discussed in this book, and practical advice is given on how to control each one.

The photographs of flowers, shrubs, trees and vegetables have been so positioned in the book that they reflect, month by month, the beauty of the garden as it changes with the seasons. For example, because azaleas are blooming in August, the photograph of the plant in bloom will be included in the pages devoted to that month.

The name by which a plant is commonly known has been used throughout the book, except where it is important that no confusion occurs, as when selecting plants for sowing or when identifying a plant in a photograph. In such cases the botanical name has been given, usually followed by the common name.

The book is deliberately repetitive to save the reader from having to page back and forth.

Gardens need regular attention if they are to look their best, and this book provides planned and constructive help for everyone from the experienced gardener to the complete novice. The reluctant gardener especially will find it a boon. By following the guidance offered, month by month, gardening will be easier, better planned and, naturally, more successful.

JANUARY

High summer and the garden is a blaze of colour, and garden competitions are being held in most towns. In the summer rainfall areas gardeners are making tentative plans for the winter garden. Small flower buds are forming on the camellias giving promise of beautiful blooms to come. It is also a reminder that, if the weather is dry, the bushes must be watered once a week from now on.

Summer flowering annuals

Remove faded flowers, and water regularly in dry weather. Feed once a month with 2:3:2 at the rate of 50 g per square metre, scattered among the plants and watered in immediately. Alternatively, feed every two weeks with a liquid fertiliser such as Multifeed P, Nitrosol or Lush. There is still time to sow alyssum, dwarf marigolds and portulaca, even where frosts are experienced.

Summer rainfall areas: Put out snail bait in the late afternoon after rain or watering.

Hardy summer flowering annuals

If these are sown now the seedlings will stand through the winter and start flowering early next summer. Best results are usually obtained from seed sown in seed trays:

Acroclinium (Helipterum)
Ageratum houstonianum (floss flower) (only in warm areas)
Agrostemma githago milas (agrostemma)
Alcea rosea (hollyhock) (annual variety)
Alyssum
Anagallis (pimpernel)
Anchusa capensis 'Blue Bird'
Antirrhinum majus (snapdragon)
Callistephus chinensis (aster)
Campanula medium (Canterbury bells)
Centaurea cyanus (cornflower)
Centaurea moschata (sweet sultan)
Clarkia
Daucus carota var. carota (white lace flower or Queen Anne's lace)
Delphinium grandiflorum (butterfly delphinium)
Dianthus (pinks)
Dianthus barbatus (sweet William)
Digitalis purpurea (foxglove)
Gaillardia pulchella (blanket flower)
Gilia capitata
Godetia (satin flower)
Iberis umbellata (candytuft)
Limonium bonduellii (statice or sea lavender)
Linum grandiflorum (flowering flax)
Lupinus hartwegii (lupin)
Malcolmia maritima (Virginian stocks)
Matricaria maritima (feverfew)
Mimulus luteus (monkey flower)
Mimulus moschatus (musk flower)
Moluccella laevis (bells of Ireland or shell flower)
Nigella damascena (love-in-a-mist)
Papaver rhoeas (Shirley poppy)
Petunia x *hybrida*
Phlox drummondii
Reseda odorata (mignonette)
Rudbeckia (gloriosa daisy)
Salpiglossis sinuata (painted tongue or trumpet flower)
Scabiosa atropurpurea (pincushion flower)
Tropaeolum majus (nasturtium) (not in very cold areas)
Verbascum phoeniceum (verbascum)
Verbena x *hybrida*

Winter flowering annuals

Prick out or transplant *Primula malacoides* (fairy primula) and ornamental kale seedlings.

Sweet peas: Prepare trenches for sweet peas. Dig a trench at least 40 cm wide and 60 cm deep, keeping the bottom soil on one side. Break up the soil at the base of the trench. Return the bottom soil, well mixed with liberal quantities of compost and/or old, well-rotted manure and 150 g of superphosphate per metre of trench. As the top soil is being returned, mix it with compost and/or old, well-rotted manure and 150 g of 2:3:2 per metre of trench. Prepare the trench in this way at least a month before sowing the seed.

A week before sowing, give the ground a light sprinkling of lime and rake this into the top layer of soil. When the ground has been prepared erect a trellis. This can consist of nylon or wire netting at least two metres wide, stretched between stout posts or attached to a wall. Those who exhibit blooms often train each plant to a separate stake. Groups of sweet peas can also be grown in small circular beds, supported by a 'wigwam' of tall stakes tied together at the top, or by a circular tube of wire netting.

Summer rainfall areas: Sow *Papaver nudicaule* (Iceland poppy), *Viola* x *wittrockiana* (pansy) and *Viola cornuta* (viola) seed.

1. Begonia semperflorens *(bedding begonias) are ideal summer bedding plants.*

2. Delphiniums, *one of the loveliest blue flowers for the summer garden.*

3. Gazania krebsiana, *real sunshine plants that flourish in well drained soil.*

Perennials

Prick out or transplant polyanthus (*Primula* x *polyantha*, sold as *P. acaulis*) and primrose (*P. veris*) seedlings.
Refrigerate the seed of 'Pacific Giant' *Delphiniums* before sowing. Buy fresh seed and place this in an airtight container in the refrigerator (not the deep freeze), for two or three weeks, and then sow.
Acanthus: Cut foliage and old flowering stems down to ground level. Mulch with compost and scatter 60 g of 2:3:2 round the root area and water in.
Chrysanthemums: Scatter a tablespoon of 2:3:2 round each clump once a month, or feed with Multifeed P, Nitrosol or Lush every two weeks at the rate recommended on the container. Tie the plants to their stakes.
Delphiniums (crowns and seedlings planted in autumn): Water copiously, protect from slugs and snails, and tie new flower stems to stakes where necessary.
Pelargoniums (geraniums): Feed with 2:3:2 once a month. Give plants growing in the open about a tablespoonful scattered over the root area, and those in pots a teaspoonful scattered over the soil. Water in immediately. In the summer rainfall areas there is a tendency for rust to attack geraniums in damp weather, so spray with any remedy which has copper oxychloride, mancozeb or triforine as the active ingredient (e.g. Cupravit, Dithane or Funginex, respectively). Pay particular attention to the undersides of the leaves. Where infection is bad remove the lower, badly affected leaves.

Staking chrysanthemums. *Place a stake close to the plant. Loosely loop soft twine or raffia round the plant and then round the stake in a 'figure of 8'. Tie a loose knot, and leave the ends of the twine or raffia quite long so that the tie can be adjusted as the plant grows bigger.*

4. *(Above)* Campanula medium *(Canterbury bells), gay summer annuals.* **5.** *(Below)* Lobelia erinus *are charming edging plants for the shadier parts of the garden.* **6.** *(Right)* Gerbera jamesonii *(Barberton daisy) flowers best if shaded during the hottest part of the day.*

7. Chrysanthemum frutescens *(Marguerites) are very rewarding as they have a long flowering season.*

8. *Stately* Agapanthus *are a feature of South African summer gardens.*

Disbudding dahlias. *When some buds are removed the plant puts its energy into the remaining buds, and the flowers that result will be finer.*

9. Cannas *(Indian shot) are invaluable for massed display and flower until the first heavy frosts.*

Bulbs

Agapanthus: Water abundantly in dry weather.

Amaryllis belladonna (March lily): If the plants have become overcrowded, lift, divide and replant the bulbs, with the neck of the bulb just below the surface of the soil. In the winter rainfall areas wait until April and lift after flowering.

Cannas: Water during dry weather, and scatter 60 g of 2:3:2 round each clump once a month. Water in after application. Remove old flower stems by gripping them firmly at the base and giving them a sharp twist.

Dahlias: Water during dry weather, and feed every two weeks with a soluble fertiliser such as Nitrosol, Multifeed P or Lush, at the rate recommended on the container. Disbud by removing all but one bud on each stem. Tie the plants to stakes and watch for red spider.

Gladioli: Water regularly. Spray once a week against thrips and gladiolus fly, and spray for rust if necessary. Lift those which are dying back.

Irises: Finish lifting and dividing the clumps this month.

Lachenalia: Start planting these South African bulbs. Plant in containers in the summer rainfall areas so that they can easily be put under cover in summer as the bulbs rot if they get too much water during their dormant season. Water sparingly in all areas until they come up.

Liliums: As the blooms fade remove the seed heads (unless the seed is to be saved), cutting them off with the minimum amount of stem. Give each clump a tablespoon of 3:1:5. Dissolve this in 5 ℓ of water, apply to the root area and water in. Keep the ground well mulched with compost.

Nerine sarniensis (Guernsey lily): Finish planting these bulbs. Watch all nerines for attack by the amaryllis caterpillar (or lily borer).

White evergreen arum lilies: If the plants are overcrowded and the flowers deteriorating they can be lifted and divided this month. Cut some of the older leaves off, then replant the tuber-like rhizomes in soil enriched with compost and a dressing of superphosphate at the rate of 200 g per square metre.

Pot plants

See *SEPTEMBER 'Caring for your pot plants'*.

Water tropical plants frequently and spray the foliage when the weather is hot and dry.
Transplant calceolaria, cineraria and primula seedlings from seed trays into small pots ('pot up'), or if they are already in pots then transfer them to a larger size pot ('pot on').
Sow seed of *Calceolaria crenatiflora* (slipper plant), *Senecio cruentus* (cineraria), *Cyclamen* and *Primula obconica*.

Shrubs

Half-ripe cuttings (of this past spring and summer's wood) of all shrubs can be taken this month.
Azaleas: Water regularly and hose down the foliage. Take half-ripe cuttings of the new growth that was sent out in spring.
Camellias: Mulch the ground under the bushes with acid compost and/or bark (obtainable from your nursery) and, from now on, water once a week if the weather is dry. This is important for bud development. It is the ideal time to take half-ripe cuttings of the new wood that was sent out in spring.
Cotton lavender: Prune lightly after the shrub has flowered.
Hydrangeas: Remove faded flowers unless they are required for flower arrangements. Give each bush 30 g of 2:3:2 and mulch with compost and/or peat. Water two or three times a week, hosing down the foliage. Watch for red spider.
Roses: Continue weekly preventive spraying against black spot, rust and mildew. Foliar feed with Seagro fish emulsion or Nitrosol, and add Kelpak 66 liquid seaweed for trace elements. Give each bush 2 tablespoons of 2:3:2 scattered over the root area. Renew the mulch of compost on the beds, and water well once a week if the weather is dry.
Scented verbena: Once this has finished flowering, prune lightly. Cut to just below the flower heads.

Climbers

Train each plant on to the trellis, pergola, wall or other surface that it is to cover. Remove faded flowers, keep the ground around the base mulched, and water if the weather is dry. Watch for pests and diseases and deal with them promptly.

Lawns

Feed with 2:3:2 once during the month at the rate of 60 g per square metre. Scatter this over the grass when it is dry, and water in immediately after application. Mow regularly, and water during dry weather, doing this in the morning.
If your lawn is infected with fungi make up a solution of Dithane (active ingredient: mancozeb) at the rate recommended on the container, and saturate the infected areas. Then aerate with an ordinary garden fork, a hollow tine fork or a spiked roller. Feed with 2:3:2 at the rate of 60 g per square metre scattering this over the infected areas.
If insects such as sodweb worms, caterpillars and giant crickets are eating the grass at night leaving bare patches, spray the insects with Wurmsprey (or any other remedy which has chlorpyrifos as the active ingredient). Alternatively, deal with sodweb worms and crickets by pouring a solution of Karbaspray (or any other insecticide that has carbaryl as an active ingredient), or a solution of household detergent, down their holes. Another way of controlling sodweb worms is to leave damp sacks on the grass at night and next morning collect up the worms that will have gathered under them.

10. *(Above)* X Ruttyruspolia, *a colourful summer flowering shrub with a long flowering season.* **11.** *(Left)* Mandevilla splendens (Dipladenia), *an exceptionally beautiful climber that likes full sun.*

Trees

Keep the ground under all trees mulched with bark and/or compost, and water well once during the month if the weather is hot and dry. If any branches have been broken by wind or hail trim them off neatly to sound wood and seal all large cuts with tree seal.

Fruit (and nuts)

Apples, pears and quinces: Spray late ripening varieties against codling moth every three weeks. Collect fallen fruit, soak and bury, or place in plastic refuse bags and throw away. As fruit is harvested give each tree 2 kg of 2:3:2, scattering this over the root area, starting at least 10 cm, and preferably about 20 cm away from the trunk and going out to just beyond the drip line of the branches.

Apples and pears must be picked before they are ripe. They are ready to harvest if the fruit comes away easily when lifted in the palm of the hand and given a slight twist. Store in a dark cupboard or in boxes until ripe. Inspect regularly when in storage.

Apricots, cherries, nectarines, peaches and plums: Spray late peaches against fruit fly. Start putting out bait to catch the last generation of fruit fly. Collect all fallen fruit, soak in water to which an insecticide has been added, then bury it. Alternatively, place the fallen fruit into a plastic refuse bag, being careful to tie the top of the bag tightly, and then dispose of it.

As the fruit is harvested give the trees their final application of fertiliser for the season. Scatter 2 kg of 2:3:2 evenly over the root area, starting at least 10 cm away from the trunk and going out to just beyond the drip line of the branches. Give cherry trees only 1 kg of 2:3:2 each. Spray for pear slug after the fruit has been harvested.

Berries: Give boysenberries, youngberries and raspberries 60 g of 3:1:5 per metre of row, scattering this over the soil, starting 10 to 12 cm away from the stems of the plants. Renew the mulch, train new canes to their supports and water during dry weather. Raspberries in particular must never lack moisture.

12. *A lovely display of* Delphiniums *and* Digitalis purpurea *(foxgloves) in a summer garden.*

Fruit that ripens in January

Apples: Alma; Winter Banana.
Grapes: Agawani (December into January); Cardinal; Dan-Ben-Hannah (from mid January); Muscat Ottonel; Muska; Niagra (White Catawba); Queen of the Vineyard (December into January).
Peaches: Elberta; Elberta Cling (mid January); Imperani (early January); Kakamas (mid to end of January); Professor M.M. Black (early January onwards); Professor J. Neethling (early January onwards).
Pears: Clapp's Favourite; December Pear (December into January); Le Conte; Bon Chretien.
Plums: Eldorado (early January); Gaviota (these keep well); Greengage; Mariposa; Red Ace (mid January); Santa Rosa (December into January); Wickson.

Citrus: Water every three weeks during dry weather.
Grapes: Spray for mildew if necessary. Grapes never ripen once they have been picked, so always sample a berry or two before cutting a bunch.
Guavas: Water thoroughly every two weeks during dry weather.

Mangoes: Apply 2 kg of 3:1:5, scattering this over the root area, starting at least 10 cm away from the trunks of the trees and going out to just beyond the drip line of the branches.
Mulberries: Water once during the month if the weather is exceptionally dry.
Pawpaws: Water every two weeks during dry weather.
Strawberries: Water once a week during dry weather.
Other fruits: Water well during dry weather.

Vegetables

Feed vegetables once a month. Either scatter 2:3:2 along the rows at the rate of 60 g per metre, or apply a liquid fertiliser such as Multifeed P or Nitrosol at the rate recommended on the container. Water before and after applying any fertiliser. Water vegetables regularly as they should never suffer a check. Keep the ground between the rows mulched with compost. Pull up weeds by hand. Pick beans twice a week and spray tomatoes once a week against early and late blight.

These vegetables can be sown in the various regions this month:

Transvaal and OFS Highveld

Beetroot; Celeriac (finish sowing); Dwarf bean (finish sowing); Endive; Globe artichoke; Jerusalem artichoke (plant tubers); Lettuce; Parsnip; Radish; Swede turnip (swede); Swiss chard; Turnip.

Transvaal Middleveld

Endive; Globe Artichoke; Jerusalem artichoke (plant tubers); Parsnip; Radish; Swede turnip (swede); Swiss chard; Turnip; Vegetable marrow (finish sowing).

Transvaal Lowveld and warm frost-free areas

Capsicum (pepper); Eggplant (aubergine, brinjal); Pumpkin; Sweet potato (finish planting).

OFS and Northern Cape

Beetroot; Broccoli; Brussels sprouts; Cabbage (main sowing); Carrot; Cauliflower (main sowing); Celeriac; Celery; Dwarf bean (finish sowing); Leek; Lettuce; Parsnip; Pumpkin (finish sowing); Runner bean (finish sowing); Swede turnip (swede); Swiss chard; Tomato; Turnip.

Natal Midlands

Beetroot; Broccoli (finish sowing); Brussels sprouts; Cabbage (main sowing); Cauliflower; Celeriac (finish sowing); Dwarf bean (finish sowing); Endive; Leek; Lettuce (Cos); Parsley (finish sowing); Parsnip; Peas; Radish; Runner bean (finish sowing); Swiss chard; Turnip.

Eastern Cape and Karoo

Beetroot; Cabbage (finish sowing); Carrot; Cauliflower (finish sowing); Dwarf bean (finish sowing); Lettuce; Swiss chard.

Western Cape: Winter rainfall areas

Broccoli; Brussels sprouts; Cabbage (finish sowing); Cauliflower (finish sowing); Dwarf bean (finish sowing); Lettuce; Parsley; Radish; Runner bean (finish sowing).

FEBRUARY

This is usually a busy month in the garden. In many parts of the country gardeners will be busy sowing winter flowering annuals. Most of the summer flowering annuals will go on flowering for some time if the faded blooms are removed promptly, and if the plants are fed from time to time and watered regularly when the weather is dry. Red spider can be troublesome during hot, dry weather, so watch carefully for the telltale yellow stippled leaves. Snails are active in the summer rainfall areas and can only be kept under control if bait is put out regularly at night.

13. Antirrhinum majus *(snapdragons), superb in the garden and as cut flowers.*

14. Digitalis purpurea *(foxglove).*

Annuals

Summer flowering annuals

Remove faded flowers, and water regularly in dry weather. Feed once a month with 2:3:2 at the rate of 50 g per square metre scattered among the plants and watered in immediately. Alternatively, feed every two weeks with a liquid fertiliser such as Multifeed P, Nitrosol or Lush.

Hardy summer flowering annuals

Any of the annuals listed below that were not sown in January can still be sown this month. Best results are usually obtained from seed sown in seed trays. If these annuals are sown now the seedlings will stand through the winter and start flowering early next summer:

Acroclinium (Helipterum)
Ageratum houstonianum (floss flower) (only in warm areas)
Agrostemma githago milas (agrostemma)
Alcea rosea (hollyhock) (annual variety)
Alyssum
Anagallis (pimpernel)
Anchusa capensis 'Blue Bird'
Antirrhinum majus (snapdragon)
Callistephus chinensis (aster)
Campanula medium (Canterbury bells)
Centaurea cyanus (cornflower)
Centaurea moschata (sweet sultan)
Clarkia
Daucus carota var. carota (white lace flower or Queen Anne's lace)
Delphinium grandiflorum (butterfly delphinium)
Dianthus (pinks)
Dianthus barbatus (sweet William)
Digitalis purpurea (foxglove)
Gaillardia pulchella (blanket flower)
Gilia capitata
Godetia (satin flower)
Iberis umbellata (candytuft)
Limonium bonduellii (statice or sea lavender)
Linum grandiflorum (flowering flax)
Lupinus hartwegii (lupin)
Malcolmia maritima (Virginian stocks)
Matricaria maritima (feverfew)
Mimulus luteus (monkey flower)
Mimulus moschatus (musk flower)
Moluccella laevis (bells of Ireland or shell flower)
Nigella damascena (love-in-a-mist)
Papaver rhoeas (Shirley poppy)
Petunia x *hybrida*
Phlox drummondii
Reseda odorata (mignonette)
Rudbeckia (gloriosa daisy)
Salpiglossis sinuata (painted tongue or trumpet flower)
Scabiosa atropurpurea (pincushion flower)
Tropaeolum majus (nasturtium) (not in very cold areas)
Verbascum phoeniceum (verbascum)
Verbena x *hybrida*

Winter flowering annuals

Sweet peas: These can be sown at the end of the month in all areas. A week before sowing, give the ground a light sprinkling of lime and rake this into the top layer of soil. Erect the trellis before sowing.

Summer rainfall areas: Any of the annuals listed below can be sown from the *beginning of the month* onwards, unless otherwise stated:

Winter rainfall and warm frost-free areas: Any of the annuals listed below can be sown from the *middle of the month* onwards, unless otherwise stated:

Calendula officinalis (pot marigold)
Chrysanthemum carinatum (annual variety)
Clarkia
Consolida ambigua (larkspur) (sow in situ)
Dorotheanthus bellidiformis (Mesembryanthemum criniflorum) (Livingstone daisy or Bokbaaivygie) (protect seedlings from birds by putting chicken wire over the beds)
Lathyrus odoratus (sweet pea) (sow at end of month in all areas)
Linaria maroccana (toad flax) (sow in situ)
Lupinus hartwegii (lupin) (sow in situ)
Matthiola incana (stocks) (sow at end of month in all areas)
Nemesia
Papaver nudicaule (Iceland poppy)
Phacelia
Schizanthus (poor man's orchid)
Ursinia anethoides (jewel of the veld)
Venidium fastuosum (Aus daisy or bitter gousblom)
Viola cornuta (viola)
Viola x *wittrockiana* (pansy)

Note: Wait until next month to sow *Dimorphotheca sinuata* (Namaqualand daisy). If sown when the weather is still hot they are liable to be attacked by a fungus.

15. Dianthus x allwoodii, *easy to grow and they flower well.*

Perennials

Seedlings of seed sown in November and December should be large enough to plant out into the garden now.
Take cuttings of *Centaurea cineraria* (Dusty Miller), *Chrysanthemum frutescens* (marguerites) and penstemons. Follow the same procedure as described for geraniums.
Delphiniums: Water copiously and cut down old flower stems.
Dianthus and carnations: These can be propagated now by layering. (See the illustration below.)
Hellebores: These are probably starting to bud. Give the plants about a heaped tablespoon of 2:3:2 scattered round each plant, and mulch with compost. Start watering regularly if the weather is dry. Put out snail bait round the plants if necessary.
Pelargoniums (geraniums): Start pruning. Cut zonal and regal pelargoniums back by half, and trim ivy leafed pelargoniums if they are becoming too spreading. The tips of prunings can be used for cuttings. The cuttings should be about 7 to 8 cm long. Cut just below a node or leaf joint. Trim off the lower leaves, and dip the end of each cutting in a rooting hormone such as Seradix No. 2. Insert the cutting in sand, and firm in, then water.

Layering carnations. *It is a good idea to replace carnations after their second year, and this is easily done by layering. In layering, a stem attached to a plant is induced to root. Once rooted the stem is cut, producing a separate new plant.*
1. *Choose a vigorous side shoot and strip off the lower leaves, leaving about 5 pairs of developed leaves at the tip. Use a small knife to cut through the stem below the lowest leaves and through the joint below.* **2.** *Twist the knife and cut through one side of the stem just below the joint, leaving a tongue which opens away from the parent plant.* **3.** *Bend the stem down towards the ground, and then bend it up from the cut. Press the cut into the soil and peg it into place.* **4.** *Once the layered stem has made its own roots – after about 6 weeks – sever the stem from the parent plant.*

Taking cuttings of chrysanthemums
1. *Choose healthy shoots about 6 cm long, and cut them off about 1 cm above the soil.*
2. *Cut the stem just below the bottom leaf joint. Remove the two lower leaves. Dip the end of the stem into rooting hormone powder before planting.*

Pricking out seedlings. *Seedlings are 'pricked out' or transplanted from the tray, pot or bed in which they were raised, to give them more room to grow. Once the first leaves have appeared, prepare the new tray, pot or bed with the same compost as that in which the seedlings have been growing. Make a hole in the soil with the dibber, lift the seedling gently, and place it in the hole. Firm the soil round the plant with the fingers. Space the seedlings about 5 cm apart and water with a fine spray.*

16. *(Left)* Gaillardia aristata *(blanket flower), an extremely hardy and rewarding garden flower.* **17.** *(Above)* Gypsophila elegans *(baby's breath), a dainty flower that mixes well with other annuals in the garden and with cut flowers.*

18. Impatiens oliveri *does best in subtropical gardens as this species is tender to frost.*

Summer flowering bulbs

Agapanthus: Water abundantly in dry weather.
Amaryllis belladonna (March lily): Before flowering, in the summer rainfall areas, if the plants have become overcrowded, lift, divide and replant the bulbs, with the neck of the bulb just below the surface of the soil. In the winter rainfall areas lift in April, after flowering.
Cannas: Water during dry weather, and scatter 60 g of 2:3:2 round each clump once a month. Water in after application. Remove old flower stems by gripping them firmly at the base and giving them a sharp twist.
Dahlias: Water during dry weather, and feed every two weeks with a soluble fertiliser such as Nitrosol, Multifeed P or Lush, at the rate recommended on the container. Disbud by removing all but one bud on each stem. Tie to stakes and watch for red spider.
Gladioli: Water regularly, spray once a week against thrips and gladiolus fly, and spray for rust if necessary. Lift those which are dying back.
Liliums: As the blooms fade remove the seed heads (unless the seed is to be saved), cutting off the heads with the minimum amount of stem. Give each clump a tablespoon of 3:1:5 dissolved in 5 ℓ of water. Apply this to the root area and water in. Keep the ground well mulched with compost.
White evergreen arum lilies: If the plants are overcrowded and were not lifted last month they can still be lifted and divided this month. Cut off some of the older leaves, and then replant the tuber-like rhizomes in soil enriched with compost and a dressing of superphosphate at the rate of 200 g per square metre.

Planting bulbs under trees. *Bulbs can be successfully grown under large trees if a special bed is prepared using heavy plastic sheeting as a base.*

In the chosen spot dig a hole about 40 cm deep, removing all the small tree roots. Leave the larger roots undisturbed but remove the soil around them. Drape plastic sheeting over the roots, moulding it to their shape and to the contours of the hole.

Cut a few drainage holes at the lowest parts of the plastic, and refill the hole with prepared soil. The bed is now ready for planting.

19. *(Above)* Nerine filifolia, *being such dainty plants, are specially attractive when massed.* **20.** *(Below)* Nerine sarniensis *sparkles in the sun as though dusted with gold.*

21. Hedychium coccineum *(red ginger lily), fragrant as well as beautiful.*

Winter flowering bulbs

These bulbs can be planted now:

Amaryllis belladonna (March lily) (plant now only in the summer rainfall areas)
Gladiolus blandus
Gladiolus carinatus (mauve Afrikander)
Ipheion uniflorum (star of Bethlehem)
Lachenalia (Cape cowslip) (in the summer rainfall areas plant these in pots which can be moved under cover because the fleshy little bulbs rot easily if they get too wet in summer)
Veltheimia bracteata (V. viridifolia) (forest lily)

If winter flowering bulbs have been left in the ground apply a dressing of 3:1:5 at the rate of 60 g per square metre. Water the fertiliser in well. Renew or apply a mulch of compost spreading a 5 cm layer evenly over the ground.
Prepare beds and pots for planting other winter flowering bulbs next month. Dig in plenty of well-matured compost and 60 g of superphosphate per square metre. Do not use manure now, but keep any which you have for mulching the beds after planting.

Pot plants

See *SEPTEMBER 'Caring for your pot plants'*.
Continue feeding and watering achimenes, amaryllis (*Hippeastrums*), tuberous rooted begonias and caladiums.
Transplant primula, cineraria and calceolaria seedlings from seed trays into small pots ('pot up'). If they are already in pots and are outgrowing them then transfer each seedling to a larger size pot ('pot on').
If cyclamens have become pot bound, either repot or replace the top soil. Water sparingly.
Finish sowing calceolaria seed by the middle of the month. Continue sowing cyclamen seed.

Lawns

Continue feeding once a month with 2:3:2 at the rate of 60 g per square metre. Scatter this over the grass when it is dry, then water in immediately.

Mow regularly and water if the weather is dry. Deal with fungi, caterpillars and crickets as soon as you notice them.

Shrubs

Keep the ground mulched with compost and water once every three weeks during hot dry weather. Pay special attention to watering camellias and azaleas. Hose down azaleas once a week in dry windy weather. If azalea foliage is turning yellow apply iron chelate at the rate recommended on the container, plus a tablespoon of magnesium sulphate (Epsom salts) per bush, and acidify the soil with pine needles, acid peat or a light dusting of sulphur.
Roses: Continue preventive spraying against black spot, rust and mildew combining this with a foliar feed such as Seagro fish emulsion or Nitrosol. Water once a week during dry weather.

Climbers

Train plants to their supports as they grow. Water every three weeks during dry weather and keep the ground mulched with compost.

Trees

Water once a month during dry weather and keep the ground mulched with coarse compost.

Fruit (and nuts)

Apples, almonds, apricots, cherries, grapes, nectarines, peaches, pears, plums and quinces: Once the fruit has been harvested give trees and vines their final application of fertiliser. Give all of these deciduous fruits, except almonds and grapes, 2 kg of 2:3:2 scattered over the root area. Water in well. Give almonds and grapes only 1,5 kg of 2:3:2.

As the leaves start falling rake them up and put them on the compost heap.

Continue to put out bait for fruit fly. Trees which have been attacked by pear slug should be sprayed with Karbaspray as soon as the fruit has been harvested.
Litchis: After the fruit has been harvested give each tree 500 g of 3:1:5 scat-

22. Antigonon leptopus *(coral creeper), a glorious sight when in full flower.*

Four Hibiscus rosa-sinensis. **23.** *'Apple Blossom' bears large dark throated flowers of apple-blossom pink.* **24.** *An attractive yellow hibiscus.* **25.** *'Camdenii', a lovely variety with large single scarlet blooms.* **26.** *'Eldorado', a striking semi-double golden-yellow variety.*

tered over the root area. Apply the 3:1:5 to damp soil and start at least 10 cm away from the trunk. Water in after application.
Pawpaws: Give each tree 125 g of LAN (limestone ammonium nitrate). Scatter this over the root area starting at least 10 cm away from the stem.
Pecans: Water thoroughly once a month.
Pineapples: Apply 60 g of 2:3:2 scattered along per metre of row.
Strawberries: Prepare the bed now for planting in April. Dig in plenty of old, well-rotted manure and/or compost, then scatter on 3:1:5 at the rate of 250 g per square metre.

Vegetables

Continue to feed summer vegetables still producing good crops. Either scatter 2:3:2 along the rows at the rate of 60 g per metre, or apply a liquid fertiliser such as Multifeed P or Nitrosol at the rate recommended on the container. Water before and after applying any fertiliser.
Continue to water vegetables regularly. Pull up any which have finished bearing. Transplant the seedlings of winter vegetables (broccoli, Brussels sprouts, cabbage, cauliflower, kohlrabi and Swiss chard) as soon as they are large enough. Do not let any get too tall ('leggy') or too old and 'woody' in the seed trays. Transplant the seedlings when about 7 to 9 cm tall. Water every four or five days during dry weather. Spray tomatoes once a week against blight.

These vegetables can be sown in the various regions this month:

Transvaal and OFS Highveld

Beetroot; Brussels sprouts (finish sowing); Cabbage; Carrot; Cauliflower (finish sowing); Dwarf spinach; Endive; Globe artichoke; Jerusalem artichoke (plant tubers); Kohlrabi; Leek; Lettuce; Onion; Parsnip; Radish; Swede turnip (swede) (finish sowing); Swiss chard; Turnip.

27. *An attractive shrub border with interesting contrasts of colour and texture.*

Transvaal Middleveld

Beetroot; Brussels sprouts; Cabbage (finish sowing); Carrot; Cauliflower (finish sowing); Dwarf bean (finish sowing); Dwarf spinach; Endive; Kohlrabi; Leek; Lettuce; Onion; Parsnip; Radish; Swede turnip (swede); Swiss chard; Turnip.

Transvaal Lowveld and warm frost-free areas

Beetroot; Brussels sprouts; Cabbage; Capsicum (pepper); Carrot; Cauliflower; Celeriac; Celery; Dwarf bean; Dwarf spinach; Eggplant (aubergine, brinjal); Horseradish (plant cuttings); Onion; Radish; Runner bean; Swede turnip (swede); Swiss chard; Tomato; Turnip.

OFS and Northern Cape

Beetroot; Broccoli (finish sowing); Brussels sprouts (finish sowing); Cabbage (finish sowing); Carrot; Cauliflower (finish sowing); Celeriac; Celery (finish sowing); Endive; Leek (finish sowing); Lettuce; Onion; Parsnip; Swiss chard.

Natal Midlands

Beetroot; Brussels sprouts (finish sowing); Cabbage; Carrot; Cauliflower (late varieties); Celery; Dwarf bean (finish sowing); Endive; Kohlrabi; Lettuce; Onion; Peas; Radish; Swiss chard; Turnip.

Eastern Cape and Karoo

Broccoli; Carrot; Cauliflower (late varieties); Leek; Lettuce; Radish; Swede turnip (swede); Swiss chard; Turnip.

Western Cape: Winter rainfall areas

Beetroot; Broccoli; Brussels sprouts; Cabbage; Carrot; Cauliflower (late varieties); Celery; Dwarf bean; Leek; Lettuce; Onion; Parsley; Parsnip; Radish; Runner bean; Spinach; Turnip.

Herbs

Seeds of anise, caraway, coriander, dill and fennel may be starting to ripen and the plants must be watched so that the seed can be gathered before it falls.

MARCH

Now is the time to think about planting winter flowering bulbs. Even the smallest garden can have a drift of daffodils if the bulbs are planted in groups and not in straight rows. The indigenous bulbs (sparaxis, ixia, babiana) look particularly effective planted in groups under deciduous trees. Start sowing Namaqualand daisies, Ursinias and Bokbaaivygies in sunny places in the garden. They grow easily and make a magnificent mass display.

28. *Summer annuals look charmingly natural when planted in informal massed groups.*

Pinching back sweet pea seedlings
When sweet peas are about 10 cm tall pinch back the growing tip above the second or third pair of leaves to encourage the formation of vigorous side growths. Allow only two of the new stems to develop.

Annuals

Summer flowering annuals

Water those which are still flowering. Pull up those which have come to the end of their flowering season and prepare the beds for winter flowers by digging in well-matured compost and 2:3:2 at the rate of 60 g per square metre.

Hardy summer flowering annuals

Continue sowing these in the winter rainfall and warm frost-free areas. Best results are usually obtained from seed sown in seed trays. If they are sown now the seedlings will stand through the winter and start flowering early next summer:

Acroclinium (Helipterum)
Ageratum houstonianum (floss flower)
Agrostemma githago milas (agrostemma)
Alcea rosea (hollyhock) (annual variety)
Alyssum
Anagallis (pimpernel)
Anchusa capensis 'Blue Bird'
Antirrhinum majus (snapdragon)
Callistephus chinensis (aster)
Campanula medium (Canterbury bells)
Centaurea cyanus (cornflower)
Centaurea moschata (sweet sultan)
Clarkia
Daucus carota var. carota (white lace flower or Queen Anne's lace)
Delphinium grandiflorum (butterfly delphinium)
Dianthus (pinks)
Dianthus barbatus (sweet William)
Digitalis purpurea (foxglove)
Gaillardia pulchella (blanket flower)
Gilia capitata
Godetia (satin flower)
Iberis umbellata (candytuft)
Limonium bonduellii (statice or sea lavender)
Linum grandiflorum (flowering flax)
Lupinus hartwegii (lupin)
Malcolmia maritima (Virginian stocks)
Matricaria maritima (feverfew)
Mimulus luteus (monkey flower)
Mimulus moschatus (musk flower)
Moluccella laevis (bells of Ireland or shell flower)
Nigella damascena (love-in-a-mist)
Papaver rhoeas (Shirley poppy) (sow in situ)
Petunia x *hybrida*
Phlox drummondii
Reseda odorata (mignonette)
Rudbeckia (gloriosa daisy)
Salpiglossis sinuata (painted tongue or trumpet flower)
Scabiosa atropurpurea (pincushion flower)
Tropaeolum majus (nasturtium)
Verbascum phoeniceum (verbascum)
Verbena x *hybrida*

Winter flowering annuals

Summer rainfall areas: In the warmer parts of these areas sow:

Arctotis acaulis
Calendula officinalis (pot marigold)
Chrysanthemum carinatum (annual variety)
Clarkia
Consolida ambigua (larkspur) (sow in situ)
Dimorphotheca sinuata (Namaqualand daisy)
Dorotheanthus bellidiformis (Mesembryanthemum criniflorum) (Livingstone daisy or Bokbaaivygie) (protect seedlings from birds by covering beds with chicken wire)
Felicia bergerana (kingfisher daisy)
Godetia (satin flower)
Linaria maroccana (toad flax) (sow in situ)
Nemesia
Schizanthus (poor man's orchid)

Winter rainfall and warm frost-free areas: In these areas sow:

Arctotis acaulis
Calendula officinalis (pot marigold)
Chrysanthemum carinatum (annual variety)
Clarkia
Consolida ambigua (larkspur) (sow in situ)
Dimorphotheca sinuata (Namaqualand daisy)
Dorotheanthus bellidiformis (Mesembryanthemum criniflorum) (Livingstone daisy or Bokbaaivygie) (protect seedlings from birds by covering beds with chicken wire)

Felicia bergerana (kingfisher daisy)
Godetia (satin flower)
Lathyrus odoratus (sweet pea)
Linaria maroccana (toad flax) (sow in situ)
Nemesia
Viola x *wittrockiana* (pansy)

Pansies: Do not over-water seedlings, but keep the soil evenly damp.
Sweet peas: Do not over-water seedlings, but keep the soil evenly damp. When seedlings are about 10 cm tall pinch them back, then allow only two of the new stems to develop.

Two Verbena x hybrida. **29.** *This brilliant red verbena makes a striking ground cover in a sunny spot.* **30.** *A colourful verbena for edgings or massed bedding.*

31. Zinnia elegans *(zinnia), very popular summer bedding plants.*

Perennials

Water once a week during dry weather. As the flowers fade cut the stems down to ground level.
In the summer rainfall areas water hellebores once a week.
Lifting perennials: The following perennials can either be lifted and divided now, or in September when new growth has started. Water the clumps the day before they are to be lifted. After lifting do not let the roots become dry. Do the dividing in the shade, and if you are expecting the task to take some time cover the clumps with damp sacking to further protect the roots. For replanting choose healthy young growths from the outer edge of the clump.

Ajuga reptans (bugle mint)
Alyssum saxatile
Anemone japonica
Anthemis sancti-johannis
Armeria maritima (thrift)
Aster novi-belgii (Michaelmas daisy)
Campanula
Chrysanthemum maximum (shasta daisy)
Echinacea purpurea (pink rudbeckia)
Gaillardia x *grandiflora* (blanket flower)
Geum
Heuchera sanguinea (coral bells)
Lobelia cardinalis (not in very cold areas)
Macleaya cordata (plume poppy)
Monarda didyma (bee balm or bergamot)
Penstemon
Pyrethrum roseum
Salvia farinacea (blue salvia)
Salvia patens (dark blue salvia)
Solidago (golden rod)
Veronica (speedwell)

Lifting and dividing overgrown perennials. *A large tough clump of perennials can be divided more easily by using two forks. Insert the forks into the clump, back to back, then force the roots apart by pushing the handles of the forks towards each other.*

Taking cuttings: Cuttings of the following perennials can be taken this month. Select healthy growths, about 5 cm long, and cut just below a node or leaf joint. Remove the lower leaves, and dip the end of the cutting in a rooting hormone. Then insert the cutting in sand, or a mixture of 2 parts sand and 1 part peat. Press the soil firmly round the cutting, and water.

Alyssum saxatile
Centaurea cineraria (Dusty Miller)
Chrysanthemum frutescens (marguerite)
Heliotropium arborescens (heliotrope or cherry pie)
Pelargonium (geranium)
Penstemon

Water features

Remove fallen leaves from fish ponds.

Bulbs

Summer flowering bulbs

Agapanthus: Water abundantly in dry weather. If the plants have become overcrowded, lift, divide and replant them. Do not split the clumps into very small pieces, otherwise they take a long time to flower again.
Brodiaea laxa: If these are planted now they will flower in early summer.
Cannas: Water during dry weather, and scatter 60 g of 2:3:2 round each clump once a month. Water in after application. Remove old flower stems by gripping them firmly at the base and giving them a sharp twist.
Dahlias: Water during dry weather, and feed every two weeks with a soluble fertiliser such as Nitrosol, Multifeed P or Lush, at the rate recommended on the container. Disbud by removing all but one bud on each stem. See that the plants are securely tied to their stakes. Check the labels to make sure that the names are correct and legible. Replace old labels that are getting hard to read with new flexible self-tie shrub labels. Use a waterproof pen when writing the names. A little time spent on labels now can prevent a lot of guesswork next season.
Day lilies (Hemerocallis) and summer flowering red-hot pokers (Kniphofias): These can be lifted and divided if the clumps have become overcrowded.
Gladioli: Water regularly, spray once a week against thrips and gladiolus fly, and spray for rust if necessary. Lift those which are dying back.
Liliums: As the blooms fade remove the seed heads (unless the seed is to be saved), cutting the heads off with the minimum amount of stem. Give each clump a tablespoon of 3:1:5 dissolved in 5 ℓ of water. Apply this to the root area and water in. Keep the ground well mulched with compost.
White evergreen arum lilies: If the plants are overcrowded and were not lifted last month they can still be lifted and divided this month. Cut off some of the older leaves, and then replant the tuber-like rhizomes in soil enriched with compost and a dressing of superphosphate at the rate of 200 g per square metre.

32. Amaryllis belladonna *(March lily), a must for every garden.*

33. Crocosmia masonorum *does well in semi-shade and makes a fine display in autumn.*

Winter flowering bulbs

If not planted last month these bulbs can still be planted now:

Gladiolus blandus
Gladiolus cardinalis (waterfall gladiolus)
Gladiolus carinatus (mauve Afrikander)
Gladiolus tristis (night scented yellow gladiolus)
Ipheion uniflorum (star of Bethlehem)
Lachenalia (Cape cowslip) (in the summer rainfall areas plant these in pots which can be moved under cover because the fleshy little bulbs rot easily if they get too wet in summer)
Veltheimia bracteata (V. viridifolia) (forest lily)

As soon as the weather gets cooler the following bulbs can also be planted:

Allium neapolitanum
Anemone coronaria
Aristea thyrsiflora (tall aristea)
Babiana
Bulbinella floribunda (cat's tail)
Dipidax triquetra (star of the marsh)
Iris (Dutch iris)
Freesia
Hyacinthus orientalis (hyacinth or Dutch hyacinth)
Ixia (wand flower or corn lily)
Leucojum (snowflake)
Lycoris radiata (spider lily)
Muscari botryoides (grape hyacinth)

Narcissus (daffodil, jonquil and bunch-flowered narcissus)
Ornithogalum thyrsoides (chincherinchee)
Ranunculus asiaticus (ranunculus)
Schizostylis coccinea (river lily)
Sparaxis (harlequin flower)
Tritonia

Pot plants

See *SEPTEMBER 'Caring for your pot plants'.*
Feed amaryllis (*Hippeastrums*), achimenes and tuberous rooted begonias.
Increase the water supply to cyclamen.
Plant daffodils, narcissi, jonquils and hyacinth bulbs in pots ('pot up') for winter.
Feed primulas, cinerarias and calceolarias once during the month with Pokon, Seagro fish emulsion or Nitrosol, and water regularly. Any seedlings that have not yet been transplanted from seed trays into small pots should be 'potted up' now.

Lawns

Continue feeding once a month with 2:3:2 at the rate of 60 g per square metre. Scatter this over the grass when it is dry, then water it in immediately. Water once a week during dry weather and mow regularly. Where grass was attacked by fungi during the summer, saturate the lawn with Bordeaux mixture to prevent the same thing happening next summer.

Shrubs

Keep the ground mulched with compost and water once every three weeks during hot dry weather. Pay special attention to watering camellias and azaleas.
Azaleas: Hose these down frequently in dry windy weather. If the foliage is turning yellow apply iron chelate at the rate recommended on the container, plus a tablespoon of magnesium sulphate (Epsom salts) per bush, and acidify the soil with pine needles, acid peat or a light dusting of sulphur.
Roses: Give each bush 2 tablespoons of 3:1:5 spread over the root area to harden up the new growth for winter. Continue spraying against black spot, rust and mildew, using Benlate or Funginex. Foliar feed by spraying the bush with Seagro fish emulsion or Nitrosol.

34. Justicia brandegeana *'Yellow Queen': this yellow form of the shrimp plant is a lovely sight when in full flower.*

Climbers

Remove any dead branches or faded flowers. Spray if you notice any pests or diseases. Water well every two to three weeks if the weather is hot and dry.
Mandevilla laxa: Remove the seed pods for the sake of tidiness. Remove any dead wood.

Trees

Remove any dead branches and faded flowers. Spray if you notice any pests or diseases. Water well every two to three weeks if the weather is hot and dry.

Fruit (and nuts)

Where necessary give trees and vines their final application of fertiliser for the season. As a general rule give mature trees 1,5 kg of 2:3:2. Spread this over the root area, then water it in well. Continue putting out bait for fruit fly.
Bananas: Give each plant 30 g of 3:1:5 scattered over the root area. Mulch the ground with compost.
Citrus: Give each tree 2 kg of 3:1:5 and 75 g of magnesium sulphate (Epsom salts). Scatter both over the root area. Water thoroughly every three weeks if the weather is dry.

35. *An imaginative way to use pot plants.*

Grapes: Give each vine 1 kg of LAN (limestone ammonium nitrate).
Loquats: Give each tree 2 kg of 2:3:2 scattered over the root area. Mulch the ground with compost.
Mangoes: Give each tree 2 kg of 3:1:5 scattered over the root area. Mulch the ground with compost.
Pawpaws: Give each tree 125 g of LAN (limestone ammonium nitrate) scattered over the root area, but starting at least 10 cm away from the stem.
Pecans: Water thoroughly once a month.

Strawberries: If not done last month prepare the bed now for planting next month. Dig in plenty of old, well-rotted manure and/or compost. Then scatter on 3:1:5 at the rate of 250 g per square metre.

Fruit that ripens in March

Apples: Delicious; Golden Delicious; Ohenimuri; Rome Beauty; Russet; Starking; Starspur; Versfeld's (Rymer).
Grapes: Barbarossa; Barlinka; Isabella (Catawba); Seneca.
Pears: Florelle (starts ripening); Winter Nellis.

Vegetables

Continue watering and caring for the last of the summer vegetables. Keep the ground between the rows mulched with compost. Pull weeds up by hand. Water the early winter vegetables, such as Brussels sprouts, broccoli, cabbage and cauliflower, that were sown in December. Feed them with 2:3:2 at the rate of 30 g per metre of row, or give them Lush, Multifeed P, Nitrosol or Seagro fish emulsion at the rate recommended on the container.
Tomatoes: Spray once a week against blight, using Dithane (active ingredient: mancozeb), Antracol (active ingredient: propineb), or any fungicide which has copper oxychloride as the active ingredient.

These vegetables can be sown in the various regions this month:

Transvaal and OFS Highveld

Beetroot; Carrot; Dwarf spinach; Endive (finish sowing); Garlic (plant

36. *A charming corner featuring dwarf conifers and colourful annuals.*

cloves); Kohlrabi; Leek; Lettuce; Onion; Parsnip; Radish; Swiss chard; Turnip.

Transvaal Middleveld

Beetroot; Carrot; Dwarf spinach; Endive (finish sowing); Garlic (plant cloves); Kohlrabi; Leek; Lettuce; Onion; Parsnip; Radish; Swede turnip (swede); Swiss chard; Turnip.

Transvaal Lowveld and warm frost-free areas

Beetroot; Brussels sprouts; Cabbage (main sowing); Capsicum (pepper); Carrot; Cauliflower (main sowing); Celeriac; Celery; Cucumber; Dwarf bean; Dwarf spinach; Eggplant (aubergine, brinjal); Endive; Garlic (plant cloves); Horseradish (plant cuttings); Kohlrabi; Leek; Lettuce; Onion; Parsley; Parsnip; Peas; Pumpkin; Radish; Runner bean; Swede turnip (swede); Swiss chard; Tomato; Turnip; Vegetable marrow (all types).

OFS and Northern Cape

Beetroot; Carrot; Dwarf spinach; Endive; Lettuce; Onion; Parsnip; Radish; Swede turnip (swede); Swiss chard; Turnip.

Natal Midlands

Cabbage; Carrot; Cauliflower; Celery; Dwarf spinach; Endive (finish sowing); Garlic (plant cloves); Kohlrabi; Leek; Lettuce; Onion; Parsnip; Swiss chard; Turnip.

Eastern Cape and Karoo

Carrot; Celery; Dwarf spinach; Leek; Lettuce; Onion; Peas; Radish; Swede turnip (swede); Swiss chard; Turnip.

Western Cape: Winter rainfall areas

Beetroot; Broad bean; Broccoli; Brussels sprouts; Cabbage; Carrot; Cauliflower; Celery; Dwarf spinach; Leek; Lettuce; Onion; Parsley; Parsnip; Peas; Radish; Swiss chard; Turnip.

Herbs

Gather the seeds of anise, caraway, coriander, dill and fennel as they ripen.

37. *Stone edging and dainty plants lend a special charm to this small bed.*

APRIL

The weather is lovely all over the country at this time of the year. Seed sowing has come to an end in all but the warm frost-free areas and even here sowing should be over by the end of the month. Gardeners who have planted clumps of the African gladiolus will now be enjoying a magnificent display of tall orange flowers.

Annuals

Summer flowering annuals

These are rapidly coming to an end and when they are past their best it is advisable to pull them up and put them on the compost heap.

Hardy summer flowering annuals

The seedlings of seed sown in seed trays in January and February should be large enough to plant out into the garden. Space them well apart and plant in groups for best effect.

Winter flowering annuals

Seed of *Dimorphotheca sinuata* (Namaqualand daisy) can still be sown in all areas.
Warm frost-free areas: Seed of the following can still be sown in seed trays:

Arctotis acaulis
Calendula officinalis (pot marigold)
Chrysanthemum carinatum (annual variety)
Clarkia
Consolida ambigua (larkspur) (sow in situ)
Dorotheanthus bellidiformis (*Mesembryanthemum criniflorum*) (Livingstone daisy or Bokbaaivygie) (protect seedlings from birds by covering beds with chicken wire)
Felicia bergerana (kingfisher daisy)
Godetia (satin flower)
Lathyrus odoratus (sweet pea)
Linaria maroccana (toad flax) (sow in situ)
Nemesia
Schizanthus pinnatus (poor man's orchid)
Viola x *wittrockiana* (pansy)

Transplant seedlings out into the garden as soon as they are large enough, about 3 cm high. Never let any, especially stocks, get too tall ('leggy') or too old ('woody') in the pans.
Sweet peas: Retain just two new shoots per plant and tie these to the trellis regularly. Remove tendrils and side shoots to encourage the main stems to grow more vigorously and produce good blooms. The tendrils are not needed by the plant, and side shoots will only produce inferior blooms.

Taking cuttings of carnations and dianthus
1. *Cut off a side shoot with about four pairs of leaves.* **2.** *Remove the lowest pair of leaves.* **3.** *Place the shoot on a folded newspaper to minimise bruising, and cut the stem cleanly just below the joint from which the lower leaves were removed.* **4.** *Place the cutting in sandy soil up to the base of the next pair of leaves. Water.*

Perennials

As blooms fade cut the flowering stems down to ground level, and remove old leaves. Mulch with compost. Water about every three weeks in the summer rainfall areas.

Lifting perennials: The perennials listed below, if not lifted last month can still be lifted and divided now, or in September when new growth has started. Water the clumps the day before they are to be lifted. After lifting do not let the roots dry. Do the dividing in the shade, and, if you are expecting the task to take some time, cover the clumps with damp sacking to further protect the roots. For replanting choose healthy young growths from the outer edge of the clump.

Ajuga reptans (bugle mint)
Alyssum saxatile
Anemone japonica
Anthemis sancti-johannis
Armeria maritima (thrift)
Aster novi-belgii (Michaelmas daisy)
Campanula
Chrysanthemum maximum (shasta daisy)
Echinacea purpurea (pink rudbeckia)
Gaillardia x *grandiflora* (blanket flower)
Geum
Heuchera sanguinea (coral bells)
Lobelia cardinalis (not in very cold areas)
Macleaya cordata (plume poppy)
Monarda didyma (bee balm or bergamot)
Penstemon
Pyrethrum roseum
Salvia farinacea (blue salvia)
Salvia patens (dark blue salvia)
Solidago (golden rod)
Veronica (speedwell)

Carnations and dianthus: Take cuttings from non-flowering basal shoots. The cuttings should be about 4 to 5 cm long. Cut just below a node or leaf joint. Remove a few lower leaves and insert the cutting in sand, or two parts sand and one part soil. Press the soil firmly around each cutting, and water.
Hellebores: In the summer rainfall areas water once a week.
Primroses and polyanthus: Never let these lack water. Work some compost and/or peat in around the point where the leaves and the roots meet (the 'crown'), as it is from this point that the plants put out new roots.
Violets: Apply a light dressing of 2:3:2 at the rate of 60 g per square metre. Mulch with sifted compost. Start watering once a week in the summer rainfall areas.

Bulbs

Summer flowering bulbs

As long as dahlias and cannas are flowering water them about once a week if the weather is dry. Water liliums and evergreen bulbous plants such as agapanthus, red hot pokers and day lilies about every three weeks when the weather is dry.
Continue lifting evergreen agapanthus, day lilies and summer flowering red hot pokers if they are overcrowded.
Brodiaea laxa: If these are planted now they will flower in early summer.
Hostas: Before the foliage dies down use small stakes to mark the spot where each plant was growing.
Winter rainfall areas: If March lilies have finished flowering and if the clumps have become overcrowded, lift, divide and replant the bulbs, with the neck of the bulb just below the surface of the soil.

Winter flowering bulbs

Continue planting all these listed below. Tulips that have not been kept in cold storage ('untreated' tulips) can also be planted now.

Allium neapolitanum
Anemone coronaria
Aristea thyrsiflora (tall aristea)
Babiana
Bulbinella floribunda (cat's tail)
Dipidax triquetra (star of the marsh)
Iris (Dutch iris)
Freesia
Hyacinthus orientalis (hyacinth or Dutch hyacinth)
Ipheion uniflorum (star of Bethlehem)
Ixia (wand flower or corn lily)
Leucojum (snowflake)
Lycoris radiata (spider lily)
Muscari botryoides (grape hyacinth)
Narcissus (daffodil, jonquil and bunch-flowered narcissus)
Ornithogalum thyrsoides (chincherinchee)
Ranunculus asiaticus (ranunculus)
Schizostylis coccinea (river lily)
Sparaxis (harlequin flower)
Tritonia
Tulip ('untreated' bulbs)

38. Gladiolus x hortulanus: *the modern gladiolus hybrids are magnificent both as garden plants and cut flowers.* **39.** Kniphofia praecox *(red hot poker), striking and bold especially when massed.*

Pot plants

Stop feeding all pot plants except calceolarias, cinerarias, cyclamen, primulas and winter flowering bulbs.
Water all pot plants, except those mentioned above, less frequently as the weather gets cooler. Never let them dry out, however. This is important especially for ferns and orchids. As the foliage of amaryllis (*Hippeastrums*), achimenes, tuberous rooted begonias, caladiums and gloxinias starts dying back, gradually reduce watering.

Lawns

Grass no longer needs feeding now. Mow if necessary in the winter rainfall and warm frost-free areas.
Water the grass once a month in the summer rainfall areas.

Shrubs

Take hardwood cuttings: These must be of fully mature wood which developed in the past spring or early summer. The cuttings should be about 20 cm long after the immature tips have been removed. Cut just below a node or leaf joint. Remove the leaves from the bottom two thirds of each cutting.

Root the cuttings in the open ground. Make a V-shaped trench in the garden about 15 cm deep and put a thin layer of sand at the bottom. Dip the end of each cutting into a rooting hormone such as Seradix No. 3 (for hardwood cuttings) and then position the cutting in the trench. Fill the trench with soil, firm in well, then water.

In the summer rainfall areas keep the soil damp, but not saturated, during winter and early spring until the summer rains start. The cuttings should be ready to plant in their permanent position in the garden in the winter or early spring of next year.
Summer rainfall areas: Water shrubs from the winter rainfall areas about once a week. These include ericas, leucadendrons, leucospermums and proteas, etc. Water camellias and azaleas once a week, and other shrubs about once a month. Keep the ground round shrubs mulched with compost or bark.

Climbers

Start taking hardwood cuttings. Follow the same procedure as described above under *Shrubs*.
Summer rainfall areas: Water about once a month.

Trees

Take hardwood cuttings. Follow the same procedure as described above under *Shrubs*.
Summer rainfall areas: Water well about once a month and mulch with coarse compost or bark.

40. Senecio tamoides *(canary creeper) makes a brilliant splash of colour in autumn.*

41. Barleria obtusa *(bush violet), a tender evergreen that bears colourful flowers.*

42. Tecomaria capensis *(Cape honeysuckle), an attractive indigenous plant which can be grown as specimen, wall shrub or hedge.*

43. Berberis thunbergii atropurpurea *makes an attractive dwarf hedge of red-bronze foliage.*

44. Abutilon x hybridum *(Chinese lantern) flowers right through summer.*

45. Cotoneaster frigida *is a handsome shrub when decked with brilliant red berries.*

46. Holmskioldia sanguinea *(Chinese hat plant) is an ideal wall shrub.*

Fruit (and nuts)

Put out bait for fruit fly as the last generation overwinters in evergreens and the flies come out to feed on fine days.
Almonds: Give each tree 1 kg of 2:3:2 scattered over the root area. Start at least 10 cm away from the trunk and work out as far as the drip line of the branches.
Citrus: Water well every three weeks in dry weather.
Guavas: Give each tree 2 kg of 2:3:2 scattered over the root area. Start at least 10 cm away from the trunk and work out as far as the drip line of the branches. Water during dry weather.
Mangoes: Water regularly from now on.
Pecans: Water thoroughly once a month in the summer rainfall areas.
Strawberries: Plant, and then water once a week during dry weather.

Vegetables

Pull up all summer vegetables that have finished bearing. Put healthy plants on the compost heap, but never do this with unhealthy plants. Give all members of the cabbage family (broccoli, Brussels sprouts, cabbage, cauliflower and kale) a light dressing of LAN (limestone ammonium nitrate). Dissolve a tablespoon in 5 ℓ of water and apply to a metre of row. Water before and after application.
Warm frost-free areas: As soon as tomato seedlings come up start spraying once a week against blight.

These vegetables can be sown in the various regions this month:

Transvaal and OFS Highveld

Broad bean; Dwarf spinach; Garlic (plant cloves); Kohlrabi; Leek; Lettuce; Parsnip; Radish; Swiss chard; Turnip.

Transvaal Middleveld

Broad bean; Dwarf spinach; Garlic (plant cloves); Kohlrabi; Leek; Lettuce; Parsnip; Peas; Swiss chard; Turnip.

Transvaal Lowveld and warm frost-free areas

Beetroot; Broad bean; Brussels sprouts; Cabbage (main sowing); Capsicum (pepper); Carrot; Celeriac; Celery; Cucumber; Dwarf bean; Dwarf spinach; Eggplant (aubergine, brinjal); Endive; Garlic (plant cloves); Horseradish (plant cuttings); Kohlrabi; Leek; Lettuce; Parsley; Parsnip; Peas; Pumpkin; Radish; Runner bean; Swede turnip (swede); Swiss chard; Tomato; Turnip; Vegetable marrow (all types).

OFS and Northern Cape

Broad bean; Carrot; Dwarf spinach; Garlic (plant cloves); Peas; Radish; Swede turnip (swede); Turnip.

Natal Midlands

Broad bean; Carrot; Dwarf spinach; Garlic (plant cloves); Kohlrabi; Leek; Lettuce; Parsnip; Radish; Swede turnip (swede); Turnip.

Eastern Cape and Karoo

Broad bean; Garlic (plant cloves); Onion; Peas; Radish.

Western Cape: Winter rainfall areas

Beetroot; Broad bean; Cabbage; Carrot; Celery; Dwarf spinach; Endive; Garlic (plant cloves); Kohlrabi; Leek; Lettuce; Onion; Parsley; Parsnip; Peas; Radish; Swede turnip (swede); Swiss chard; Turnip.

Herbs

Continue to gather the seeds of anise, caraway, coriander, dill and fennel. Always collect the seed when the weather is dry.

47. *Lavender adds colour and scent to the herb garden.*

48. *Herbs make an attractive border.*

MAY

Time to think of winter protection where heavy frosts are experienced. In the summer rainfall areas, as there is now no prospect of rain for the next eight months, start watering shrubs, roses, fruit trees and vines. Many shrubs and trees are showing their autumn colours. The stately Liquidambars are rich crimson with touches of scarlet, the Tulip tree and the Maidenhair tree are pure gold this month, and in some districts the apricot trees and Lombardy poplars are now a golden yellow. But perhaps the most spectacular tree of all in autumn is the Wax tree with its almost indescribable display of colours.

Annuals

Hardy summer flowering annuals

Water once a week during dry weather and feed once a month with a liquid fertiliser such as Nitrosol, Lush or Seagro fish emulsion, to maintain steady growth. Water in the morning in areas that experience frost, so that the foliage has time to dry before nightfall.

Winter flowering annuals

Feed twice a month with a liquid fertiliser such as Nitrosol, Lush or Seagro fish emulsion. Remove faded flowers regularly, especially from Iceland poppies, pansies and violas. Water during dry weather, doing this in the morning in areas that experience frost.

Larkspur and stocks: If the lower leaves turn yellow this is a sign of nitrogen deficiency. To remedy this give the plants a dressing of LAN (limestone ammonium nitrate). Dissolve 60 g of LAN in 5 ℓ of water and apply to a square metre. Do this once a month for two to three months, or until the plants are healthy and green again. Water before and after application.
Sweet peas: Tie the plants to their stakes or trellis as they grow, and remove tendrils and side shoots so that nutrients are not wasted on unnecessary growth. Increase the water supply as the plants grow. Water at least once a week in the summer rainfall areas.

Cutting down dahlias. *As soon as the foliage has died back, cut the stems down to 15 to 20 cm.*

Storing dahlias in boxes. *One way of storing dahlia tubers for winter is to place them in boxes. After lifting, wash the soil off the tubers, and allow to dry. Place the tubers in the boxes and cover with peat or sand. Store in a shed. Water lightly from time to time.*

A bare rooted plant.

A plant grown in a black plastic nursery bag.

Perennials

Tidy up plants as they die down, removing old flower stems and dead leaves. Mulch with compost and water once a month in the summer rainfall areas. Where plants were attacked by mildew during summer, spray thoroughly with Funginex or Fungisprey.
Anemone japonica, Michaelmas daisy and physostegia can still be lifted this month if they are overcrowded.
Hellebores: In the summer rainfall areas water once a week.

Bulbs

Summer flowering bulbs

Cannas: Once the foliage has died back, cut the stems down to ground level. In areas that experience frost cover the plants with a deep mulch of coarse compost to protect the rhizomes.
Dahlias: As soon as the foliage has died down, cut the stems down to 15 to 20 cm. Tie all labels securely to the stems. If the tubers are to be left in the ground in the summer rainfall areas cover them with a deep mulch of coarse compost.

If the tubers are to be lifted and stored for winter, first cut off the tails by pushing a sharp spade down vertically into the ground about 15 cm from the stems, then lift carefully. The tubers can then be placed in a trench in the garden and covered with soil.

If they are to be stored in boxes wash the soil off, place the tubers in the boxes, cover with peat or sand, and then store them in a shed. Water lightly from time to time during winter. Do not store the tubers without any covering as they will shrivel and be of no use next season.
Liliums: When the foliage has died down, cut the stems off and cover the plants with compost. Mark their positions with a ring of small stakes.
Summer rainfall areas: Water agapanthus, day lilies (*Hemerocallis*) and liliums at least once a month.

Winter flowering bulbs

As the bulbs come up water more frequently, about once a week in the summer rainfall areas. Water narcissi, daffodils and other exotic bulbs which have not yet come up, about twice a month.

Warm frost-free areas: These bulbs can still be planted:

Allium neapolitanum
Anemone coronaria
Aristea thyrsiflora (tall aristea)
Babiana
Bulbinella floribunda (cat's tail)
Dipidax triquetra (star of the marsh)
Freesia
Hyacinthus orientalis (hyacinth or Dutch hyacinth)
Ipheion uniflorum (star of Bethlehem)
Iris (Dutch iris)
Ixia (wand flower or corn lily)
Leucojum (snowflake)
Lycoris radiata (spider lily)
Muscari botryoides (grape hyacinth)
Narcissus (daffodil, jonquil and bunch-flowered narcissus)
Ornithogalum thyrsoides (chincherinchee)
Ranunculus asiaticus (ranunculus)
Schizostylis coccinea (river lily)
Sparaxis (harlequin flower)
Tritonia

In all areas plant liliums and 'treated' tulips. 'Treated' bulbs are those which have been kept in cold storage to simulate the cold conditions these bulbs would normally have experienced in Europe, their country of origin.

Convallaria (lily of the valley): Lift and replant this month if the plants have become overcrowded and the quality of the flowers is deteriorating.

Pot plants

Feed calceolarias, cinerarias, cyclamen, daffodils, hyacinths, jonquils, narcissi, poinsettias and primulas every two weeks with Seagro fish emulsion, Pokon, Nitrosol or Lush. Water about every three days or whenever the soil feels dry.

Discontinue feeding other pot plants if this has not already been done. Water less frequently, but never let the plants, especially ferns, orchids and philodendrons, become completely dry.

Once the foliage of amaryllis *(Hippeastrums)*, caladiums, achimenes and tuberous rooted begonias has died down, reduce watering to a light sprinkling from time to time to prevent the soil becoming bone dry.

Shrubs

Hardwood cuttings that were not taken last month can still be taken now. Follow the same procedure as described in *APRIL* under *Shrubs*.

Protecting from frost: In areas where frost is experienced it is necessary to provide winter protection for tender shrubs such as proteas, beloperones, cupheas, daturas, fuchsias, hibiscus, poinsettias, etc.

Small shrubs can be covered with large cardboard boxes. To protect large shrubs place four stakes round each shrub and drape hessian over these every night all through winter. Remove the boxes and hessian covers every morning.

Protect the roots by covering the ground around the plant with a deep mulch (7 to 8 cm) of compost or bark.

Summer rainfall areas: Water azaleas, camellias and all shrubs from the winter rainfall areas once a week.

Climbers

Hardwood cuttings that were not taken last month can still be taken now. Follow the same procedure as described in *APRIL* under *Shrubs*.

In areas where frost is experienced it is necessary to protect tender plants such as bougainvilleas, abutillons, allamandas, mandevilla splendens (dipladenia), etc.

Summer rainfall areas: Water plants about once a month.

Lawns

Winter rainfall and warm frost-free areas: Mow if necessary.

Summer rainfall areas: Water the grass about once a month.

49. Platycodon grandiflorus *(balloon flower) grows best in semi-shade.*

50. Cassia corymbosa *does best in the warmer parts of the country.*

51. Crataegus x grignonensis, *one of the most colourful shrubs in autumn when decked with bright red berries.*

Trees

Hardwood cuttings that were not taken last month can still be taken now. Follow the same procedure as described in *APRIL* under *Shrubs.*

Summer rainfall areas: Water well about once a month.

Fruit (and nuts)

Put out bait for fruit fly. The last generation overwinters in evergreens and the flies come out on fine days to feed.

Order fruit trees, vines and berries to be planted 'ex open ground' (or 'bare rooted') in July. Prepare the holes for the trees and vines, and the trenches for the berries. 'Ex open ground' or 'bare rooted' plants are supplied by nurseries that specialise in fruit trees. If buying in quantity it is usually more satisfactory to buy direct from these nurseries. The plants are called 'bare rooted' because they are dug up at the nursery and then transported without soil. A substance such as peat is dampened and packed round the roots to prevent them from drying out.

Summer rainfall areas: Start pruning fruit trees and vines. Seal all large cuts with tree seal. After pruning spray trees and vines with 'winter strength' lime sulphur (1 cup lime sulphur to 8 cups water). Spray the twigs, branches, trunk and the ground under each tree or vine thoroughly. Wait 10 days and then spray again.

Citrus: Water every three weeks if the weather is dry.

Granadillas: Give each plant 75 g of 3:1:5 scattered over the root area. Water the fertiliser in well. Mulch with compost.

Mangoes: Do not water. The trees must be kept on the dry side from now until about the end of July.

Pawpaws: Give each tree 125 g of LAN (limestone ammonium nitrate) scattered over the root area, but starting at least 10 cm away from the stem.

Summer rainfall areas: Water fruit trees, vines and berries thoroughly every three to four weeks, depending on the type of soil. Water light sandy soil more frequently than heavy clay soil. Keep the ground mulched with coarse compost.

52. Cestrum elegans, *an evergreen that flowers nearly all summer.*

53. Callistemon citrinus *'Splendens' is one of the most colourful bottlebrushes, and flowers prolifically.*

54. Crataegus pubescens forma stipulacea *(Mexican hawthorn).*

55. Coleonema pulchrum *(confetti bush) bears dainty flowers for many months.*

56. Lagerstroemia indica *(pride of India) bears blooms in mid summer in shades of purple, mauve, pink, red and white.*

Vegetables

Water vegetables regularly during dry weather. Feed with Nitrosol or Multifeed P every two weeks to improve the flavour of the vegetables.
In warm frost-free areas spray tomatoes once a week against blight.
Asparagus: Prepare trenches. Before preparing the trench clear the ground of perennial weeds such as couch grass. Dig trenches any convenient length but remember that the crowns must be spaced 45 cm apart. Make the trench 45 cm wide and 25 to 30 cm deep. Break up the ground at the bottom of the trench then return the soil, mixing it well with plenty of sifted compost and/or old, well-rotted manure and a dressing of 2:3:2 at the rate of 120 g per metre of trench.

These vegetables can be sown in the various regions this month:

Transvaal and OFS Highveld

Broad bean; Lettuce; Peas; Radish; Turnip.

Transvaal Middleveld

Broad bean; Lettuce; Peas.

Transvaal Lowveld and warm frost-free areas

Beetroot; Broad bean; Cabbage; Carrot; Celery; Cucumber; Dwarf bean; Dwarf spinach; Eggplant (aubergine, brinjal); Endive; Kohlrabi; Lettuce; Parsley; Parsnip; Peas; Pumpkin; Radish; Runner bean; Swede turnip (swede); Swiss chard; Tomato; Turnip; Vegetable marrow (all types).

OFS and Northern Cape

Carrot; Garlic (plant cloves); Peas; Radish.

Natal Midlands

Broad bean; Kohlrabi; Leek.

Eastern Cape and Karoo

Broad bean; Garlic (plant cloves); Onion; Radish.

Western Cape: Winter rainfall areas

Beetroot; Broad bean; Cabbage; Carrot; Dwarf spinach; Endive; Garlic (plant cloves); Horseradish (plant cuttings); Kohlrabi; Leek; Lettuce; Onion; Parsley; Parsnip; Peas; Radish; Swede turnip (swede); Turnip.

JUNE

The first frosts can be expected in some parts of the country this month. If you live in a frosty area keep covers handy to protect tender plants, and water the garden in the morning so that the foliage is dry before nightfall. Gardeners who are planning to plant 'bare rooted' fruit trees next month, will be well advised to start preparing the holes for them now.

57. *Iceland poppies and blue violas make a pleasing colour combination.*

58. *A beautiful massed display of 'Knee-Hi' sweet peas.*

Annuals

Hardy summer flowering annuals

Water about once a week if the weather is dry, and feed once a month with a liquid fertiliser such as Nitrosol, Multifeed P, Lush or Seagro fish emulsion to keep them growing steadily.

Winter flowering annuals

Feed twice a month with a liquid fertiliser such as Nitrosol, Lush or Seagro fish emulsion. Remove faded flowers regularly, especially from Iceland poppies, pansies and violas. Water during dry weather, doing this in the morning in areas that experience frost.

Sweet peas: If the margins of the leaves are turning pale brown and papery it is a sign of potassium deficiency. There are two ways to correct this. Dissolve either 1 level tablespoon of potassium sulphate, or 2 heaped tablespoons of 3:1:5, in 5 ℓ of water and apply to a metre of row every two weeks. Water before and after application.

Tie the plants on to the trellis regularly. Remove side shoots and tendrils, and water copiously once or even twice a week. Once the plants start flowering pick the blooms frequently to encourage them to produce more and more.

Perennials

Paeonies: Prepare the ground for planting new plants or for transplanting. They do best in rich, friable, slightly alkaline soil. If the pH of the soil is below 6,5 apply a light dressing of lime (just enough to make the surface of the soil white).

Summer rainfall areas: Water at least once a month, as root growth does not cease in winter but only slows down. Keep the ground mulched with compost.

Bulbs

All bulbous plants (including white evergreen arums): As soon as the buds appear start feeding every two weeks with Nitrosol, Lush, Multifeed P or Seagro fish emulsion. Water copiously once a week when the weather is dry, especially in the summer rainfall areas.

Convallaria (lily of the valley): Lift and divide if the plants are becoming overcrowded.

Liliums: In the summer rainfall areas water liliums once a month as they are never completely dormant.
Tulips: Inspect plants for aphids which tend to hide in the crevices of the leaves. Spray with Malathion if necessary.

Pot plants

Amaryllis (Hippeastrums), achimenes, tuberous rooted begonias and caladiums: Sprinkle lightly with water from time to time to prevent the soil becoming bone dry.
Continue to feed calceolarias, cinerarias, cyclamen, daffodils, hyacinths, jonquils, narcissi, poinsettias and primulas every two weeks with Pokon, Seagro fish emulsion or Nitrosol, and water every two or three days.
Discontinue feeding other pot plants if this has not already been done. Water less frequently, but never let the plants especially ferns, orchids and philodendrons, become completely dry.

Lawns

Warm frost-free and winter rainfall areas: Mow if necessary.
Summer rainfall areas: Water the grass once a month.

Shrubs

Protecting from frost: In areas where frost is experienced continue to provide winter protection for tender shrubs at night.

Small shrubs can be covered with large cardboard boxes. To protect large shrubs place four stakes round each shrub and drape hessian over these every night all through winter. Remove the covers every morning.

Protect the roots by covering the ground around the plant with a deep mulch (7 to 8 cm) of compost or bark.
Summer rainfall areas: Water azaleas, camellias, magnolias and all shrubs from the winter rainfall areas thoroughly once a week. Water other shrubs once a month.

Climbers

Protecting from frost: In areas that experience frost protect tender climbers such as sweet peas, bougainvilleas, mandevilla splendens etc., at night by

59. *(Above)* Matthiola incana *(stocks) with their rich spicy scent are a real joy in winter.* **60.** *(Left)* Primula x polyantha *(polyanthus) can be grown in the shadier parts of the garden in winter, or in pots.*

61. *(Left)* Cineraria *makes a magnificent display in a warm winter garden.* **62.** *(Above)* Bellis perennis *(English daisy) is a charming little flower for the winter garden.*

draping hessian over them. Remove the hessian every morning.
Summer rainfall areas: Water plants well about once a month.

Trees

In areas where heavy frost is experienced protect tender young trees at night until they have grown above frost height (i.e. above 2 m). Protect in the same way as for shrubs.
Summer rainfall areas: Water trees about once a month.

Vegetables

Continue routine care for all vegetables. Water at least once a week when the weather is dry. Feed once a month with 2:3:2 at the rate of 60 g per square metre, or with a liquid fertiliser such as Nitrosol, Multifeed P or Lush every two weeks.
In warm frost-free areas spray tomatoes once a week against blight.
Asparagus: If beds or trenches were not prepared last month do this as soon as possible. Follow the procedure described last month.
These vegetables can be sown in the various regions this month:

Transvaal and OFS Highveld

Peas; Radish; Turnip.

Transvaal Middleveld

Peas.

Transvaal Lowveld and warm frost-free areas

Cabbage; Dwarf spinach; Peas; Swede turnip (swede); Turnip.

OFS and Northern Cape

None.

Natal Midlands

None.

Eastern Cape and Karoo

Peas.

Western Cape: Winter rainfall areas

Broad bean; Broccoli; Cabbage; Carrot; Cauliflower; Endive; Leek; Lettuce; Onion; Parsley; Parsnip; Peas; Radish; Spinach; Turnip.

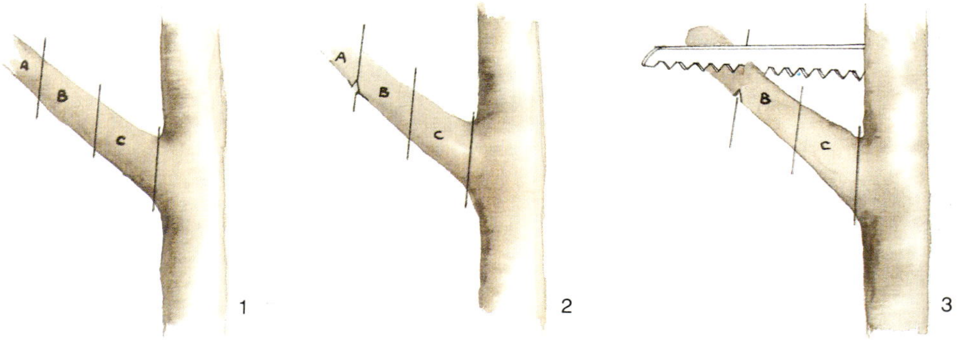

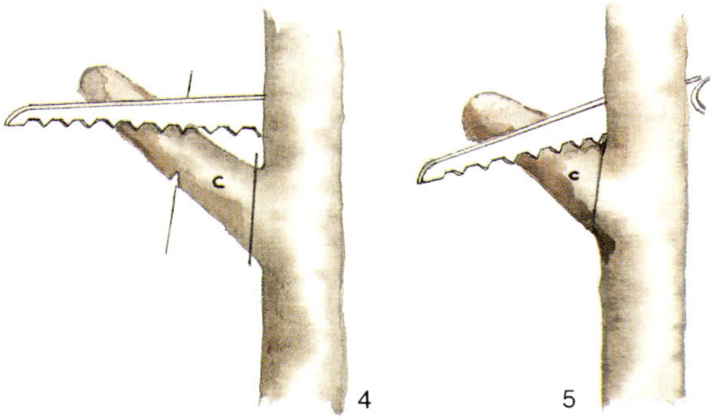

Cutting a large branch. 1. *Mark the branch off into sections (you can do this mentally).* **2.** *Start with the section furthest away from the trunk (i.e. section A), and saw a notch in the* underside *of the branch.* **3.** *Then start sawing from the top of the branch directly above the notch. Saw through the branch, joining up with the notch. This will prevent the bark from tearing.* **4.** *Repeat the same procedure on the remaining sections of branch, first cutting a notch in the underside of the branch and then sawing through from above.* **5.** *The last 2 cuts will be close to the trunk. Angle the cut so that water will run off the cut away from the trunk.*

Vase pruning fruit trees. *Pruning, when done correctly, can greatly improve the quality of the fruit that a tree produces. The method of pruning shown here is known as 'vase pruning'. The tree is shaped to a short trunk of about 1 metre, with three or four main limbs, each of which has fully filled out secondary branches. This open vase shape allows sunlight to reach the centre of the tree and all the branches. The vase pruning method may be used for apple, apricot, olive, peach, pear and plum trees.*

63. Acacia cultriformis *(knife-leaf acacia) grows to the height of a small tree and flowers in winter.*

64. Acacia podalyriifolia *(pearl acacia), a popular tree with silver-grey foliage and masses of sweetly scented yellow flowers.*

Place orders for fruit trees, grape vines and berries without delay.

Pruning: Continue to prune fruit trees and vines. Seal all large cuts with tree seal. After pruning spray trees and vines with 'winter strength' lime sulphur (1 cup lime sulphur to 8 cups water). Spray the twigs, branches, trunk and the ground under each tree or vine thoroughly. Wait 10 days and then spray again.

Citrus: Water every three weeks when the weather is dry.

Mangoes: Do not water. They need a 'stress period' before flowering.

Summer rainfall areas: Water all fruit trees, except mangoes, thoroughly once a month. Water grape vines and berries.

Pruning citrus. *Thin out citrus fruits if the branches appear overladen and in danger of breaking. Lemons, for example, tend to grow at the tips of thin branches, and so it is advisable to cut all laterals in half and pinch back new growth several times during the growing season.*

65-68. *Two lovely indigenous trees. The* Erythrina lysistemon *(above) is perfect for the small garden, while the* Erythrina caffra *(below) makes an excellent shade tree for the larger garden.*

JULY

A busy month, and time for pruning roses, fruit trees, vines and many shrubs. It is also time to think of summer flowering annuals again. The first daffodils, jonquils, and narcissi are out, anemones and ranunculus are beginning to flower, and sparaxis, ixias and babiana, Iceland poppies, stocks, calendulas, primroses and violets are all blooming. Winter need never be dull in a South African garden.

Annuals

Summer flowering annuals

Prepare seed trays now for sowing in August and September.
Begonia semperflorens (bedding begonias) and petunias: These should be sown now as the plants will take four to five months to flower. The seed trays should be kept in a warm sheltered place and protected from cold at night if the plants are to flower in time for the main summer display.

Hardy summer flowering annuals

Water once a week, especially in the summer rainfall areas, and feed once a month with Seagro fish emulsion, Lush, Multifeed P or Nitrosol.

Winter flowering annuals

Feed twice a month with Multifeed P, Nitrosol or Lush. Remove faded flowers regularly, especially from Iceland poppies, pansies and violas. Water during dry weather, doing this in the morning in areas that experience frost.
Sweet peas: If the margins of the leaves are turning pale brown and papery it is a sign of potassium deficiency. There are two ways to correct this. Dissolve either 1 level tablespoon of potassium sulphate, or 2 heaped tablespoons of 3:1:5, in 5 ℓ of water and apply to a metre of row every two weeks. Water before and after application.

Tie the plants on to the trellis regularly. Remove side shoots and tendrils, and water copiously once or even twice a week. Once the plants start flowering pick the blooms frequently to encourage plants to produce more and more.

Perennials

Paeonies: These can be planted, or lifted and transplanted this month. Plant with the 'crown' (the junction of the roots and the leaves) about 3 cm below the surface of the soil and no deeper.
Summer rainfall areas: Water hellebores once a week, and other perennials once a month.

1

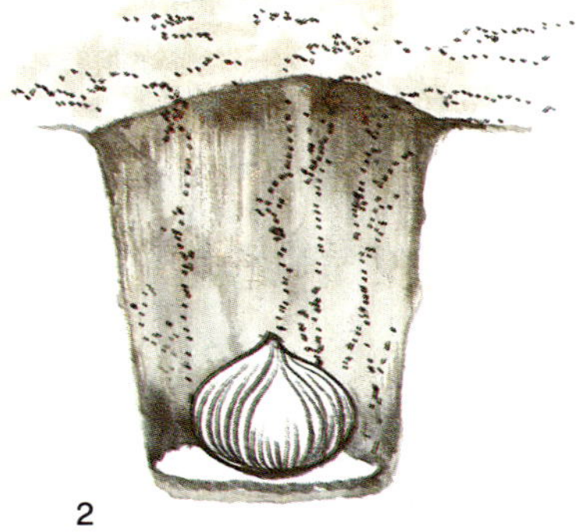
2

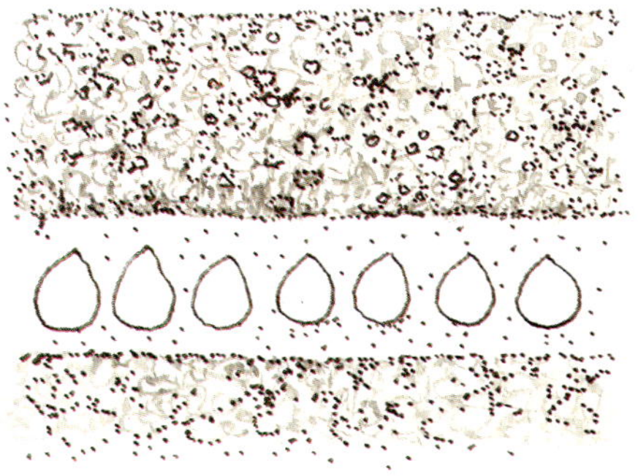
3

Planting gladioli
1. *For a beautiful garden display plant the corms in groups. Place them in a flat-bottomed hole about 12 cm deep.*
2. *Corms can also be planted in individual holes. In heavy soil, place sand in the bottom of each hole to aid drainage.*
3. *Cormlets can be planted close together in rows, in a layer of sand.*

Bulbs

Water all winter and spring flowering bulbs (anemones, daffodils, ranunculus, tulips, etc) about once a week in the summer rainfall areas.
Feed all winter and spring flowering bulbs every two weeks with Nitrosol, Multifeed P or Seagro fish emulsion.
As the flowers of daffodils, narcissi and jonquils fade, remove the flower heads only. Leave the stems so that the nutrients in them can return to the bulbs.
Agapanthus and day lilies (Hemerocallis): Water once a month in the summer rainfall areas.
Anemones: Pick regularly to encourage the plants to continue flowering.
Dahlias: Inspect dahlias in storage to make sure that no tubers are rotting and that the covering sand is slightly damp.
Gladioli: Plant the first batch. (See the illustrations.)
Liliums: In the summer rainfall areas water once a month.
Ranunculus: These need a lot of water in the summer rainfall areas.

Pot plants

Continue to feed calceolarias, cinerarias, cyclamen, daffodils, hyacinths, jonquils, narcissi, poinsettias and primulas every two weeks with Multifeed P, Nitrosol or Seagro fish emulsion. Water every two to three days.
Discontinue feeding other pot plants if this has not already been done. Water less frequently, but never let the plants, especially ferns, orchids and philodendrons become completely dry.
Amaryllis (Hippeastrums), achimenes, tuberous rooted begonias and caladiums: Water lightly from time to time to prevent the soil becoming bone dry.

Lawns

Summer rainfall areas: Water the grass once during the month.
Warm frost-free and winter rainfall areas: Mow if necessary.

Shrubs

Summer rainfall areas: Water azaleas, camellias, hydrangeas and magnolias once a week. Water all other shrubs well once during the month.
Roses: Plant 'bare rooted' roses. Unpack the parcel in the shade and put the plant/s into a bucket of water. In the prepared site open up a hole large enough to accommodate the roots comfortably and just deep enough so that the bud union will be about 2 cm below soil level. To judge what the soil

69. Muscari botryoides *(grape hyacinth), charming little spring flowers that look best when massed.*

70. Polianthes tuberosa *(tuberose) has strongly scented milk white flowers.*

level will be put a straight stick across the hole as a guide.

Make a small cone of soil in the centre of the hole and place the rose on it, making sure that the bud union is at the correct height. Hold the bush with one hand and fill in the soil, firming it down as you go. When the hole has been filled tread the soil down gently, still holding the bush at the right height. Make a shallow basin round the bush, and fill this with water. Put down a mulch of compost.

When planting standard roses remember to place the stake in the hole before positioning the plant. Place the stake just off-centre in the hole and drive it about 30 cm into the ground. The top of the stake should come about 2,5 cm above the head of the plant. Tie the standard to the stake in two places, just above the soil and just below the head of the plant. Use a 'figure of eight' tie.

Renew the ties on established standards. Prune all roses and then spray with 'winter strength' lime sulphur (1 cup lime sulphur to 8 cups water). Spray the twigs, stems and the ground under the plants quite thoroughly. Wait 10 days and then spray again.

Pruning shrubs: The shrubs listed below can be pruned this month. Prune bushes to a nice rounded shape. 'Tidying up' a plant entails removing dead wood and thin straggly stems.

Abutilon (lantern flower) (prune moderately)
Aloysia triphylla (A. citriodora) (scented verbena) (prune hard)
Barleria obtusa (prune fairly hard)
Berberis (barberry) (prune lightly to shape)
Bixa orellana (prune lightly to keep to shape and size)
Brunfelsia (yesterday-today-and-tomorrow) (prune lightly to shape and tidy up)
Buddleia davidii hybrids (butterfly bush) (prune hard)
Calycanthus floridus (Carolina allspice) (prune fairly hard)
Caryopteris incana (blue spiraea) (prune fairly hard, and remove faded flowers regularly)

Pruning a standard rose
1. *The standard before pruning. Remove any sprouting buds and any suckers that develop from the trunk or root. Prune to keep the crown symmetrical and the branches radiating evenly.* **2.** *Cut out dead or diseased branches and remove twigs from the centre. Prune the main stems by half, cutting back to a strong outward-pointing bud.* **3.** *The standard after pruning.*

71. Leptospermum scoparium *'Roseum' (Australia tea bush), a lovely winter flowering shrub.*

Cestrum (prune to keep to shape and size)
Choisya ternata (Mexican orange blossom) (prune fairly hard to shape)
Cuphea ignea (cigar flower) (prune fairly hard)
Deutzia (bridal wreath) (prune lightly to retain shape; old bushes can be pruned very hard to rejuvenate)
Dodonaea viscosa (hop bush) (prune lightly)
Duranta plumieri (golden dewdrop) (prune lightly)
Eupatorium sordidum (giant ageratum) (prune lightly)
Feijoa sellowiana (fruit salad tree) (prune lightly)
Hebe (Veronica) (prune back hard every other year to shape)
Heliotropium (heliotrope or cherry pie) (prune fairly hard)
Hibiscus sinensis (prune moderately)
Hibiscus syriacus (prune lightly to shape if necessary)
Hypericum (St. John's wort) (prune back fairly hard)
Indigofera (prune lightly)
Lavandula (lavender) (prune lightly; do not cut into old wood)
Ligustrum (privet) (prune lightly to shape)
Lonicera nitida aurea (box honeysuckle) (prune lightly to shape)
Mackaya bella (prune lightly to shape)
Malvaviscus mollis (fire dart) (prune back hard to keep to size)
Mimulus aurantiacus (prune lightly)
Myoporum laetum (ngaio) (prune lightly to keep to size and shape)
Myrtus communis (myrtle) (prune lightly to shape)
Pentas (prune hard)
Phygelius aequalis (Cape fuchsia or river bells) (prune moderately)
Plectranthus (spur flower) (prune fairly hard)
Punicia granatum 'Flore Pleno' (pomegranate) (prune moderately to shape)
Pyracantha (fire thorn) (prune moderately to shape if necessary)
Rosmarinus officinalis (rosemary) (prune moderately to shape; do not cut into old wood)
Sambucus nigra (elderberry) (prune back by about a third)
Santolina chamaecyparissus (cotton lavender) (prune moderately)
Solanum rantonettii (blue potato bush) (prune fairly hard)
Spartium junceum (Spanish broom) (prune lightly)
Spiraea albiflora (S. japonica alba) (may)
Spiraea x *bumalda* 'Anthony Waterer' (pink may)
Spiraea japonica 'Bullata' *(S. crisifolia)* (prune all these small spiraeas moderately and remove faded flowers regularly for repeat blooming)
Sutera grandiflora (wild phlox) (prune lightly)
Symphoricarpus (snow berry) (prune fairly hard)
Tecoma stans (yellow bells) (prune lightly)
Tibouchina (glory bush) (prune lightly; prune more severely in windy areas)
Viburnum carlsii (prune lightly)
Viburnum tomentosum (prune lightly to shape)

72. Anemone coronaria, *the more flowers you pick the more the plants produce.*

Climbers

Pruning: Prune these this month:
Aristolochia (Dutchman's pipe) (thin out and cut back to keep to size)
Asparagus plumosus (asparagus fern) (cut down old stems to ground level)
Clematis x *jackmanii* (prune fairly hard; the plants flower on the new wood)
Cobaea scandens (cathedral bells) (thin out and tidy up)
Cryptostegia madagascariensis (rubber vine) (prune lightly to shape and thin out)
Distictis riversii (vanilla trumpet vine) (thin out lightly if necessary)
Hibbertia scandens (H. volubilis) (Guinea gold vine) (thin out and reduce mass)
Jasminum officinale (common jasmine) (thin out and shape)
Lonicera (honeysuckle) (prune moderately to keep to size)
Mandevilla laxa (Chilean jasmine) (thin out and prune lightly; remove seed pods as soon as they form as they tend to be rather unsightly)
Manettia bicolor (prune lightly and thin out)
Maurandia barclariana (thin out and tidy up; can be cut back hard in cold areas)
Pandorea jasminoides (bower vine) (thin out; cut back long branches to prevent them sprawling and smothering nearby plants)
Parthenocissus quinquefolia (Virginia creeper) (tidy up)
Parthenocissus tricuspidata (Boston ivy) (tidy up)
Passiflora (passion flower) (prune all species fairly hard to keep under control)
Phaedranthus buccinatorius (Bignonia cherere) (Mexican blood trumpet) (thin out fairly hard)
Phaseolus caracalla (snail creeper) (thin out and tidy up)
Plumbago auriculata (P. capensis) (prune back hard; remove suckers)
Podranea brycei (Zimbabwe creeper) (thin out and cut back long branches)
Podranea ricasoliana (Port St. John's creeper) (thin out and cut back long branches)
Polygonum aubertii (silver lace vine) (prune hard)
Quisqualis indica (Rangoon creeper) (prune fairly hard)
Senecio tamoides (Canary creeper) (prune fairly hard)
Smilax (cut down old stems to ground level)
Solandra (cup of gold) (prune back hard to reduce size if encroaching on other plants)
Solanum (potato creeper) (prune back quite hard to induce new growth)
Sollya heterophylla (bluebell creeper) (thin out and shape)
Stigmaphyllon ciliatum (golden vine) (thin out lightly and shape if necessary)
Thunbergia grandiflora (sky flower) (prune fairly hard to keep under control)
Wisteria (prune back long branches to five eyes or leaf joints)

Summer rainfall areas: While the weather is dry water all climbers once a month. *Gelsemium sempervirens* (Carolina jasmine), however, should be watered once a week while in flower.

Pruning cuts: correct and incorrect

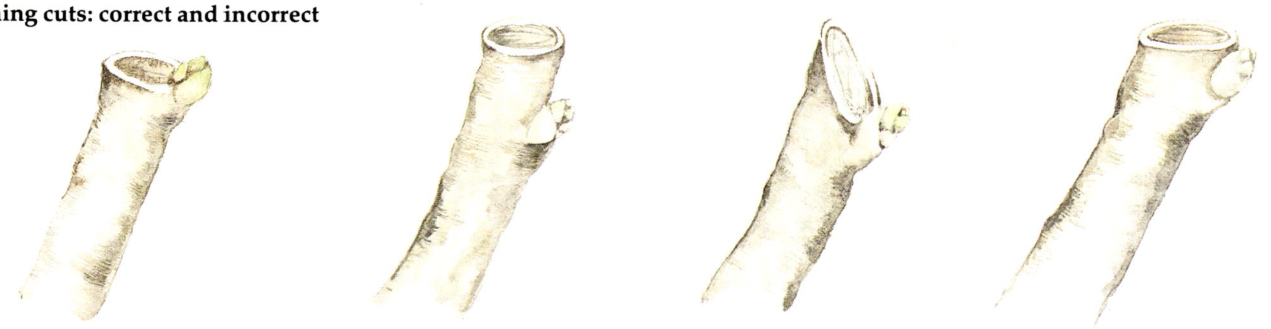

1. *Cut too close to the bud.* **2.** *Cut too far from the bud.* **3.** *This cut will damage the bud.* **4.** *Cut at the correct place and angle.*

Pruning branches

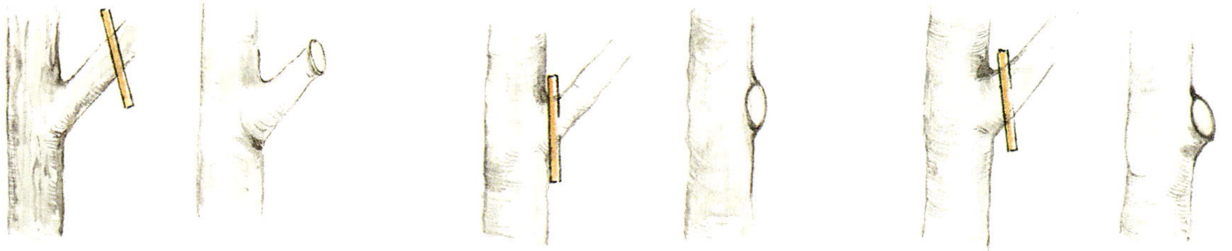

1. *Cut too far from the main stem.* **2.** *Cut too close to main stem.* **3.** *Cut at correct place and angle.*

Pruning roses: correct and incorrect cuts

1. *The cut is too slanting.* **2.** *The cut is too far away from the bud.* **3.** *The cut is too close to the bud.* **4.** *A bad jagged cut.* **5.** *Correctly cut.*

Pruning

1. *A shrub pruned* lightly. *Note the rounded shape the shrub is given.*

2. *A shrub pruned* moderately. *The shrub is cut back more than in picture 1, but the same rounded shape is maintained.*

3. *A poinsettia pruned* hard. *Hard pruning entails drastically cutting back growing shoots.*

4. *Some plants need to be pruned back extremely hard, almost to ground level.*

Trees

Summer rainfall areas: Water trees once a month.

Fruit (and nuts)

Pruning: Continue pruning deciduous fruit trees and grape vines. After pruning spray with 'winter strength' lime sulphur (1 cup lime sulphur to 8 cups water). Spray trees and vines thoroughly, covering twigs, stems and the ground around the stem. Spray again after 10 days.

Planting: Plant 'bare rooted' or 'ex open ground' fruit trees, grape vines and berries. These are plants that are dug up at the nursery and then transported without soil. A substance such as peat is dampened and packed round the roots to prevent them from drying out.

Plant 'bare rooted' fruit trees with the graft union about 10 cm above ground level or at the same depth at which the tree was growing in the nursery (look for the soil mark on the stem).

After planting, water well, then mulch the ground. If the fruit trees were not preshaped in the nursery cut them down to knee height (about 45 cm from ground level). This is the first stage in shaping the trees.

Berries: Plant 'bare rooted' boysenberries, youngberries and raspberries. Prepare a trench about 45 cm deep and 45 cm wide. Add old, well-rotted manure and/or compost, and 500 g of superphosphate per metre of trench. Space the plants 2,5 m apart. Make a hole about 7,5 cm deep in the prepared trench, spread the roots out in the hole and then cover with soil. Water well, then mulch the ground with compost. Prune plants back to 10 to 15 cm from the ground after planting.

Citrus: Give each tree 2 kg of 3:1:5 and 75 g of magnesium sulphate (Epsom salts). Scatter the fertiliser over the root area starting at least 10 cm away from the trunk. Water thoroughly every three weeks if the weather is dry.

Granadillas: Towards the end of the month prune back the long laterals (these are the long stems which hang downwards) to 60 cm from ground level. Cut back to a newly developing side shoot.

Grape vines: Plant these at the same depth at which they were growing in the nursery. Water well, then mulch the ground. Prune grape vines back to two eyes (nodes or leaf joints).

Mangoes: Give each tree 2 kg of 3:1:5 scattered over the root area starting at least 10 cm away from the trunk. Do not water until the flower panicles appear, then water thoroughly. The water must penetrate to a depth of 1,2 metres. To ensure that the trees are thoroughly watered let the hose or sprinkler run on the root area for about an hour a day for two days running.

Vegetables

Feed and water all winter vegetables at least once a week in the summer rainfall areas. When cabbages and cauliflowers have been harvested pull up the stumps as these often harbour pests if left in the ground. Chop them up and place on the compost heap.

Planting asparagus: Asparagus crowns can be planted now in all areas. Open up a trench in the site that was prepared either last month or the month before. Make a slight ridge in the centre of the trench. Place the crowns on the ridge about 45 cm apart, and spread out the roots. Fill in the trench with soil, firm lightly and water well.

These vegetables can be sown in the various regions this month:

Transvaal and OFS Highveld
Asparagus; Parsnip; Peas; Radish; Swiss chard.

Transvaal Middleveld
Asparagus; Beetroot; Parsnip; Radish; Swiss chard; Turnip.

Transvaal Lowveld and warm frost-free areas
Asparagus; Capsicum (pepper); Beetroot; Carrot; Cucumber; Eggplant (aubergine, brinjal); Globe artichoke; Jerusalem artichoke (plant tubers); Melon (all types); Swiss chard; Tomato; Vegetable marrow (all types).

OFS and Northern Cape
Asparagus; Cabbage (early varieties).

Natal Midlands
Carrot; Parsnip; Peas.

Eastern Cape and Karoo
Beetroot; Cabbage; Carrot; Cauliflower; Swede turnip (swede).

Western Cape: Winter rainfall areas
Asparagus; Beetroot; Broad bean; Brussels sprouts; Cabbage; Carrot; Cauliflower; Endive; Leek; Lettuce; Onion; Parsley; Parsnip; Radish; Spinach; Turnip.

73. Magnolia x soulangeana *is a beautiful spring flowering shrub.*

Two Camellia japonica. **74.** *(Above) 'Elegans' is a beautiful and most rewarding variety.* **75.** *(Below) One of the many pink camellias.* **76.** *(Right)* Tabebuia rosea *(rosy trumpet tree).*

Planting trees and shrubs

Trees and shrubs are permanent features in the garden and must be chosen and positioned with great care. Before planting a tree or shrub always find out what the height and spread of the plant will be when mature.

A few hours before the planting is to be done immerse the plant (still in its plastic bag) in a bucket of water for about 30 minutes. Remove from the bucket and allow to drain.

As the tree or shrub is to occupy the same position for the rest of its life it is essential that the hole be properly prepared. Prepare square holes 40 x 40 x 40 cm for shrubs, and holes 45 x 45 x 45 cm for trees. Dig out the top 20 cm of soil, and place it to one side of the hole. Then dig out the next 20 cm of soil and place it on the other side of the hole.

Break up the ground at the bottom of the hole, then replace the heap of bottom soil. Mix in 500 g of superphosphate if planting a shrub, and 1 kg of superphosphate if planting a tree. If the soil is sandy, also add a bucket or two of well-matured, sifted compost and/or peat. Replace most of the top soil, adding more compost if the soil is sandy.

Position the plant (still in its plastic bag) in the loose soil in the hole. To check that the plant will be at the right depth place a straight stick across the top of the hole. The surface of the soil in the bag should be about 2,5 cm below the stick.

Remove the plastic bag, and again position the plant in the hole.

Fill in round the plant with soil. Firm in well, but not so hard that all the air is squeezed out of the soil (especially in heavy clay soil).

Where strong winds are experienced place a sturdy pointed stake close to the plant and drive it into the soil at least 20 cm if it will be supporting a shrub, and 30 cm if supporting a tree. The stake should be long enough to come just below the head of the plant.

Tie the plant to the stake in two places: just below the head of the plant, and just above the soil. Use sisal twine and a 'figure of 8' tie.

Make a shallow basin round the plant. Fill this with water, letting the water run in slowly.

Cover the ground around the plant with a mulch of compost.

During the first 18 months to 2 years it is important to water the young tree or shrub thoroughly every 2 or 3 weeks in dry weather. In spring give shrubs 60 g of 2:3:2, and trees about 100 g of 2:3:2, scattered over the root area. Start at least 10 cm away from the stem and go out to just beyond the drip line of the branches. Always water before and after applying fertilisers. Repeat this application of 2:3:2 in mid summer. Always keep the ground around the plant mulched with compost.

Immerse the plant (still in its bag) in a bucket of water for about 30 minutes.

You will need: bucket of water; spade; hosepipe; compost and/or peat; superphosphate; possibly also sharp pointed stake and sisal twine.

Dig a square hole. Place the top soil on one side of the hole, and the bottom soil on the other.

Replace the soil from the bottom of the hole and mix in superphosphate. Replace most of the top soil.

To check that the plant will be at the right depth, place the plant (in its bag) in the loose soil in the hole. Place a straight stick across the top of the hole. The soil surface in the bag should be about 2,5 cm below the stick.

Remove the plastic bag and position the plant in the hole.

Fill in round the plant with the rest of the top soil. Firm in well.

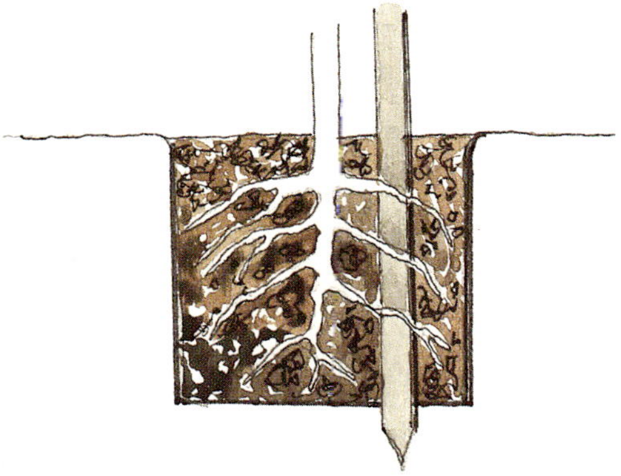

In windy areas place a stake close to the plant.

Tie the plant to the stake using a 'figure of 8' tie. Tie just below the head of the plant, and just above the soil.

Make a basin round the plant. Let the water run in slowly.

AUGUST

The winter is nearly over and the spring garden is a picture with daffodils, anemones, ranunculus, gay indigenous bulbs and spring flowering annuals. The flowering apricot will be covered with lovely pink blossoms, and possibly so will the flowering almond. And now it's time for the gardener to plan the summer garden.

Annuals

Summer flowering annuals

Prepare beds for sowing by digging in compost and 2:3:2 at the rate of 60 g per square metre.

Many summer flowering annuals can be sown this month, either at the beginning, middle or end of the month. Be guided on when to sow by the advice given below for each area.

Warm frost-free areas: All summer flowering annuals can be sown from the beginning of the month onwards.

The summer rainfall areas: Sowing can start about the middle of the month.

Where late frosts are experienced: It is advisable to delay sowing until the end of the month or the beginning of next month, or sow only under protection.

Winter rainfall areas: Wait until next month to sow, or sow only under protection.

Acroclinium (Helipterum)
Ageratum houstonianum (floss flower)
Agrostemma githago milas (agrostemma)
Alcea rosea (hollyhock)
Alyssum
Amaranthus
Anchusa capensis 'Blue Bird'
Basil 'Dark Opal'
Bidens formosa (cosmos)
Callistephus chinensis (aster)
Campanula medium (Canterbury bells)
Celosia
Centaurea cyanus (cornflower)
Centaurea moschata (sweet sultan)
Chrysanthemum carinatum
Cleome hasslerana (spider flower)
Coleus
Convolvulus tricolor (morning glory)
Cotula turbinata
Dahlia (bedding)
Daucus carota var. carota (white lace flower or Queen Anne's lace)
Dianthus (pinks)
Didiscus (blue lace flower)
Eschscholtzia californica (Californian poppy) (sow in situ)
Euphorbia variegata (snow on the mountain) (soak seed before sowing)
Gaillardia pulchella (blanket flower)
Gilia capitata
Gomphrena globosa (globe flower)
Gypsophila elegans (baby's breath)
Helianthus (sunflower)
Helichrysum (strawflower)
Impatiens balsamina (balsam)
Impatiens wallerana hybrids (busy Lizzy)
Kochia (Mexican fire bush)
Lavatera
Limonium bonduellii (statice or sea lavender)
Lobelia erinus (lobelia)
Lunaria annua (honesty)
Lupinus hartwegii (lupin)
Marigold
Matricaria maritima (feverfew)
Mimulus luteus (monkey flower)
Moluccella laevis (bells of Ireland)
Nicotiana
Nigella damascena (love-in-a-mist)
Papaver rhoeas (Shirley poppy)
Petunia
Portulaca
Reseda odorata (mignonette)
Rudbeckia hirta (gloriosa daisy)
Salpiglossis
Salvia splendens (scarlet salvia)
Scabiosa atropurpurea (pincushion flower)
Tropaeolum majus (nasturtium)
Verbena x *hybrida*
Zinnia

Hardy summer flowering annuals

The seedlings of these annuals which have stood through the winter will start growing as soon as the weather warms up. Feed them twice a month with Nitrosol, Multifeed P or Lush, at the rate recommended on the container. Water regularly during dry weather, especially in the summer rainfall areas where it is usually windy at this time of year. Mulch the ground round the plants with compost.

Winter flowering annuals

Continue to care for these. Pick the flowers regularly, especially calendulas, Iceland poppies, nemesias, pansies, primroses, sweet peas and violas. Remove faded flowers promptly. Feed about every two weeks with Multifeed P, Nitrosol or Lush and water when the weather is dry. Towards the end of the month in the summer rainfall areas some of the winter annuals may be past their prime and can be pulled up to make way for the summer annuals.

Perennials

Tidy up the plants by removing the old leaves. Mulch with compost and apply 2:3:2 at the rate of 60 g per square metre, scattering this around each clump. Begin to water about once a week if the weather is dry, to encourage new growth.

Chrysanthemums: Water the plants and as soon as the new shoots are about 7 or 8 cm long start taking cuttings.

Delphiniums: Tidy up the clumps by removing the old leaves. Mulch with compost, and feed every two weeks with Nitrosol, Multifeed P or Lush. Start watering every two weeks. Put out bait for slugs and snails in the late afternoon.

77. Babiana rubrocyanea *is an outstanding blue flowering bulb for the winter garden.*

78. Bulbinella floribunda *makes most impact when massed.*

79. Narcissus jonquilla: *their scent is the very essence of spring.*

80. Scilla peruviana *is a beautiful blue flowered scilla that prefers a sunny position.*

81. Hyacinthus orientalis *can be grown in the shady parts of the garden, or in pots indoors.*

82. Ixia campanulata *(wand flower or corn lily): dainty flowers with wiry stems that look best when massed.*

Paeonies: These can still be planted, or lifted and transplanted now. Give established plants a generous mulch of old, well-rotted manure (about 6 cm deep). If this is not available, then apply a generous mulch of compost, plus about 2 tablespoons of 2:3:2 per plant, scattering this round each clump. Start watering copiously at least once a week.

Bulbs

Winter flowering bulbs

Continue to feed daffodils, narcissi, jonquils and other bulbs which are to be kept for replanting next season. Feed with a liquid fertiliser such as Multifeed P, Nitrosol or Seagro fish emulsion. Water at least once a week. Remove faded flowers promptly.

Summer flowering bulbs

Start watching for the amaryllis caterpillar or lily borer.

Cannas: These can be lifted and replanted. They are gross feeders and need rich, well-drained soil and regular feeding during the growing season. If the rhizomes are not to be lifted, tidy up the bed, and apply a dressing of 2:3:2 at the rate of 60 g per square metre. Scatter this round the clumps. Cover the ground with a generous mulch of compost. Water every two weeks until new growth starts.

Dahlias: Start into growth by watering lightly and moving to a warm place. Then either sever the tubers with shoots and plant them, or let the shoots grow until they are 7 to 8 cm long and then take cuttings.

Gladioli: Plant batches at intervals of about four weeks.

Hedychiums (ginger lilies): Treat in the same way as cannas.

Hemerocallis (day lilies): Give each clump 2 tablespoons of 2:3:2 scattered round the clumps. Mulch with compost, and water more frequently.

Irises: Give all irises a dressing of superphosphate, the amount depending on the size of the clumps. Give small clumps about 1 tablespoon, and large clumps 2 or 3 tablespoons of superphosphate. Mulch with compost in between the clumps, and start watering once a week.

Liliums: Give each group 2 or 3 tablespoons of 3:1:5, scattered round the clumps. Cover with a generous mulch of compost (a layer 3 to 5 cm deep) to keep the roots cool. Water at least once a week if the weather is dry.

The summer flowering bulbs listed below can be planted from now on. In cold areas where late frosts are experienced, and in the winter rainfall areas, it would be advisable to wait until next month to plant the deciduous pink and yellow arums and other fleshy bulbs such as *Gloriosa superba* and *Liatris*. After planting, water thoroughly, cover the bed with compost and then water sparingly until the leaves appear.

Acidanthera bicolor
Albuca altissima
Alpinia (shell flower)
Arum (see *Zantedeschia*)
Canna (Indian shot)
Chlidanthus fragrans (Peruvian daffodil)
Colocasia (elephant ear)
Crocosmia
Cyrtanthus macowanii (Ifafa lily)
Cyrtanthus purpurea (Vallota speciosa) (Knysna or George lily)
Dahlia (start into growth)
Dietes (*Moraea*)
Eucharis grandiflora (Amazon lily)
Eucomis (pineapple lily)
Galtonia candicans (Cape hyacinth or summer hyacinth)
Gladiolus
Gloriosa superba (flame lily)
Habranthus
Haemanthus (see *Scadoxus*)
Hedychium (ginger lily)
Heliconia (lobster claw)
Hosta (protect from snails)
Hymenocallis (spider lily)
Liatris (gay feather)
Liriope (turf lily)
Montbretia
Moraea (see *Dietes*)
Nerine bowdenii
Ornithogalum saundersiae (giant flowering chincherinchee)
Polianthes (tuberose)
Polygonatum (Solomon's seal)
Scadoxus (*Haemanthus*) (paint brush lily)
Scilla natalensis
Sprekelia (Maltese cross lily)
Tigridia pavonia (one day lily)
Tulbaghia
Zantedeschia albomaculata (yellow arum)
Zantedeschia pentlandii (deep yellow arum)
Zantedeschia rehmannii (small pink arum)
Zephyranthes (storm lily)

Pot plants

As the weather gets warmer water all pot plants more frequently.

Achimenes and tuberous rooted begonias: Repot if necessary, then water sparingly about every three days until leaves show above the ground.

Aerating a lawn. *If the lawn surface is compacted, spike the soil with a fork or a wheeled aerator. This aerates the soil and allows water to penetrate.*

Amaryllis (Hippeastrums): Either remove a little of the top soil and replace with new, or completely repot the bulbs if necessary. Plant new bulbs. Water sparingly about every three days until the buds appear, then increase the water supply and start feeding every two weeks with Seagro fish emulsion, Nitrosol or Multifeed P.

Cyclamen: As the foliage starts dying down gradually reduce the water supply.

Sow seed of the following pot plants:

Asparagus ferns (all types)
Begonia rex (painted leaf)
Begonia x *tuberhybrida* (tuberous rooted)
Browallia
Capsicum (ornamental pepper)
Coleus
Exacum affine
Impatiens wallerana (busy Lizzy)
Cyclamen (if fresh seed is available)
Geranium F1 hybrids
Kalanchoe
Sinningia speciosa (gloxinia)
Solanum capsicastrum (winter cherry)
Streptocarpus (Cape primrose)
Torenia (wishbone flower) (can also be grown in shade outside)
Thunbergia alata (black-eyed Susan) (can also be grown outside)

Lawns

Give the grass its spring treatment. Scarify, removing all the old 'thatch' right down to the roots, then run the mower over the grass to cut off the stalks. Water thoroughly. Aerate with a hollow tine fork, spiked roller or garden fork. If a hollow tine fork is used remember to brush off the cores as you work.

Apply a dressing of LAN (limestone ammonium nitrate) at the rate of 60 g per square metre, and water in. Alternatively, one can also use Nitroacta, a slow release nitrogen, on the lawn. Scatter this over the grass when it is dry. Water in. Fill in hollows with sifted, weed-free, composty soil. Water again thoroughly, then do not water again until the grass has grown through the soil.

Shrubs

Give all shrubs a dressing of 2:3:2 spread over the root area. Give small shrubs 1 tablespoon, and large shrubs 2 to 3 tablespoons of 2:3:2. Mulch with compost, and water thoroughly.

Pruning shrubs: Any of the shrubs listed below that were not pruned last month can be pruned now. Prune bushes to a nice rounded shape. 'Tidying up' entails removing dead branches and thin straggly stems.

Acalypha wilkesiana (copper leaf) (prune lightly; tidy up)
Allamanda neriifolia (prune lightly)
Atriplex halimus (salt bush) (prune lightly to shape)
Aucuba japonica (Japanese laurel or gold dust) (prune to keep to shape and size)
Banksia (prune lightly to shape)
Beloperone (shrimp plant) (prune back by about a third)
Bouvardia (prune back hard)
Buddleia madagascariensis (butterfly bush)
Buddleia salvifolia (prune back by about a third after flowering)
Burchellia bubalina (wild pomegranate) (pinch back tips)
Calliandra (shuttlecock flower) (prune to keep to shape and size)

Callicarpa (beauty berry) (prune to shape if necessary)
Callistemon (bottle brush) (prune to shape if necessary; do not cut into old wood)
**Camellia* (see note)
Cantua buxifolia (flower of the Inca's) (prune to shape and to encourage new growth)
Ceratostigma (Chinese plumbago) (prune back very hard, almost to ground level)
Centradenia (prune hard)
Chimonanthus (Carolina allspice or winter-sweet) (prune fairly hard after flowering)
Chrysanthemum frutescens (marguerite) (prune to shape; do not cut the yellow variety back hard)
Clerodendrum ugandense (Oxford and Cambridge bush) (prune fairly hard to shape)
Codiaeum (croton) (prune very lightly to shape)
Coprosma (mirror plant) (prune to keep to shape and size)
Convolvulus cneorum (bush morning glory) (pinch back tips to encourage bushy growth)
Cortaderia (Pampas grass) (prune off all old plumes, and shape)
Cotoneaster (prune to shape if necessary)
Echium fastuosum (pride of Madeira) (prune lightly at beginning of the month)
Escallonia (take out straggly growth and tidy up)
Euonymus (spindle berry) (prune lightly to shape where necessary)
Euphorbia pulcherrima (poinsettia) (prune back hard)
Euryops virgineus (prune back by about a third after flowering)
Forsythia (golden bell) (cut a few old stems out each year after flowering)
Fuchsia (prune back fairly hard)
Garrya elliptica (tassle bush) (prune lightly to shape if necessary)
Holmskioldia (Chinese hat bush) (prune back long shoots)
Hydrangea (Christmas rose) (prune out old wood and thin stems; prune old flowering stems back by about a third)
Hypoestes aristata (ribbon bush) (prune back fairly hard)
Iboza (prune back by about a third after flowering)
Jasminum humile var. revolutum (jasmine) (prune lightly)
Lantana montevidensis (trailing lantana) (prune lightly to shape and tidy up)
Leonotis leonurus (lion's ear) (cut down to ground level)
Leptospermum (Australian tea bush) (prune lightly; do not cut into old wood)
Mahonia aquifolium (prune lightly to shape if necessary)
Nandina domestica (heavenly bamboo or Chinese sacred bamboo) (thin out if necessary)

***Note:** Camellias usually need little pruning but vigorous specimens may be kept in check by pruning after flowering and before new growth starts. Dense growth can be thinned out by removing straggly branches from the centre, and by shortening the remaining branches to shape the bush. If a young plant has sent out just one long stem this can be shortened by about a quarter to a third to encourage bushy growth. Old bushes can be rejuvenated by being cut back hard now.

Pinching back
1. *The size and shape of a plant, and the size and quality of the flowers, can easily be regulated by pinching back the growing tip or bud.* **2.** *Pinching induces the plant to become bushier, as it will usually produce two or three side shoots to replace the shoot that was pinched back. These side shoots can in turn also be pinched back.*

83. Forsythia x intermedia *'Spectabilis' is a delightful winter flowering shrub.*

84. Greyia sutherlandii *(mountain bottlebrush) is an attractive indigenous shrub with bright orange-red brushes.*

85. Greyia radlkoferi *(Transvaal baakhout) bears bright scarlet flowers on bare branches in winter.*

Oxypetalum caeruleum (pinch back tips to encourage bushy growth)
Russellia juncea (coral shrub) (prune lightly to tidy up if necessary)
Ruttya fruticosa (jammy mouth) (prune lightly to shape)
Senecio petasitis (cut down to ground level)
Serissa foetida (prune lightly if necessary)
Sorbaria tomentosum (false spiraea) (prune fairly hard to shape)
Spiraea arguta (garland may) (prune moderately; thin out if necessary)
Sutherlandia frutescens (Cape balloon pea) (pinch back tips to encourage bushy growth)
Viburnum burkwoodii (viburnum) (prune lightly after flowering)
Viburnum rhytidophyllum (laurel leaf viburnum) (prune fairly hard after flowering)

87. Parkinsonia aculeata *(Jerusalem thorn) with its narrow leaves and yellow flowers is an attractive tree.*

Roses: Finish pruning and spraying by the first week in the month. Spray the bushes with 'winter strength' lime sulphur. Wait 10 days and then spray again. Give each bush 2 tablespoons of 2:3:2 scattered over the root area, unless the soil is deficient in potassium, in which case use 3:1:5.

Fork the beds over lightly (do not dig any deeper than 5 cm), put down a generous mulch of compost and water thoroughly. From now on water once a week during dry weather. Check the ties on standard roses, and renew if necessary.

Summer rainfall areas: From now on water shrubs every two weeks, until the summer rains start.

86. Polygala virgata *(purple broom) is very easy to grow and the bright flower spikes show up well in the garden.*

Climbers

Give all climbers a dressing of 2:3:2, the amount depending on the size of the plant. Give small plants 30 g, and large plants 60 g of 2:3:2, scattered over the root area. Cover the root area with a mulch of compost, and water during dry weather.

Bougainvilleas: Do not water.

Pruning climbers: These climbers can be pruned this month.

Gelsemium sempervirens (Carolina jasmine) (thin out and tidy up after flowering)
Hedera helix (ivy) (tidy up if necessary)

Trees

Give each tree about 60 g of 2:3:2 spread over the root area, starting about 20 cm away from the trunk and going out to just beyond the drip line of the branches. Mulch with compost or bark.

The drip line. *When fertilising trees, spread the fertiliser over the root area. Start at least 10 cm and preferably about 20 cm away from the trunk and go out to just beyond the drip line. The drip line is an imaginary circular line directly beneath the outer perimeter of the branches.*

Pride of India (Lagerstroemia indica): Prune to shape and to encourage flowering.
Summer rainfall areas: Water all trees well once a month.

Fruit (and nuts)

Finish pruning and spraying fruit trees. Spray with 'winter strength' lime sulphur. Spray again after 10 days.
Fertilising: Fertilise apples, apricots, cherries, nectarines, peaches, pears, plums and quinces. Give each tree 2 kg of 2:3:2. Spread the fertiliser evenly over the root area, starting about 20 cm away from the trunk and going out to just beyond the drip line of the branches. Cover the ground with a generous mulch of compost.
Summer rainfall areas: Water fruit trees thoroughly every two weeks. Leave the sprinkler or hose running for about 30 minutes. Water cherries extra well once a week.
Boysenberries, youngberries and raspberries: Give each plant 2 kg of old, well-rotted manure mixed with 50 g of superphosphate per metre of row. If manure is not available substitute compost, leave out the superphosphate and instead add 60 g of 3:1:5 and a good handful of bone meal. Spread the manure or compost, mixed with the fertiliser, along the rows. In the summer rainfall areas start watering every two weeks, paying special attention to the raspberries.
Cape gooseberries: In the summer rainfall areas seed can be sown now.
Citrus: Water well every three weeks. As soon as the new leaves appear spray against citrus psylla using Dursban, Hysheen or Wurmsprey (active ingredient: chlorpyrifos) following the directions on the container.
Granadillas: Give each plant 100 g of 3:1:5 spread over the root area. Mulch with compost, and water well once a week during dry weather.
Grapes: Give each vine 2 kg of 2:3:2 and 500 g of magnesium sulphate (Epsom salts) spread over the root area. Apply the fertiliser to damp ground and water in after application. Mulch with compost, and water well every two weeks.
Litchis: Water the trees well every two or three weeks if the weather is dry.
Mangoes: Water thoroughly once during the month. To ensure that the water soaks in to a good depth water for about 30 minutes for two days running.
Mulberries: Give each tree 2 kg of 3:1:5 spread over the root area. Cover with a mulch of compost. In the summer rainfall areas water well every three weeks.
Pawpaws: Give each tree 125 g of LAN (limestone ammonium nitrate) spread over the root area.
Pineapples: Apply 3:1:5 at the rate of 60 g per metre of row. Be careful not to get the fertiliser on the foliage because it burns. Water after application.
Strawberries: Water at least once a week if the weather is dry.

Vegetables

Continue to care for the last of the winter vegetables. Water regularly and apply a liquid fertiliser such as Nitrosol, Multifeed P or Seagro fish emulsion, every two weeks. Pull up the stumps of cabbages, cauliflowers, Brussels sprouts and broccoli. As the ground is cleared prepare the beds for the summer vegetables by digging in compost and 2:3:2 at the rate of 60 g per square metre. Use 3:1:5 for tomatoes and root crops.
Tomatoes: As soon as plants come up start spraying against blight. Continue to spray once a week for the whole season.

These vegetables can be sown in the various regions this month:

Transvaal and OFS Highveld

Asparagus; Beetroot; Capsicum (pepper); Carrot; Dwarf bean; Dwarf spinach; Eggplant (aubergine, brinjal); Horseradish (plant cuttings); Lettuce (Cos); Peas; Radish; Runner bean; Swiss chard; Tomato; Vegetable marrow (all types).

Transvaal Middleveld

Asparagus; Beetroot; Capsicum (pepper); Dwarf bean; Dwarf spinach; Eggplant (aubergine, brinjal); Horseradish (plant cuttings); Lettuce (Cos); Melon (all types); Parsnip; Pumpkin; Radish; Runner bean; Swiss chard; Tomato; Vegetable marrow (all types).

Transvaal Lowveld and warm frost-free areas

Asparagus; Capsicum (pepper); Carrot; Cucumber; Dwarf bean; Eggplant (aubergine, brinjal); Globe artichoke; Jerusalem artichoke (plant tubers); Melon (all types); Parsley; Pumpkin; Radish; Runner bean; Swiss chard; Vegetable marrow (all types).

OFS and Northern Cape

Asparagus; Beetroot; Capsicum (pepper); Carrot; Dwarf bean; Dwarf spinach; Eggplant (aubergine, brinjal); Garlic (plant cloves); Kohlrabi; Parsley; Peas; Radish; Runner bean; Swede turnip (swede); Tomato; Turnip; Vegetable marrow (all types).

Natal Midlands

Asparagus; Beetroot; Carrot; Celery; Dwarf bean; Dwarf spinach; Eggplant (aubergine, brinjal); Horseradish (plant cuttings); Lettuce (Cos); Parsley; Parsnip; Peas; Runner bean; Swede turnip (swede); Swiss chard; Tomato; Turnip; Vegetable marrow (all types).

Eastern Cape and Karoo

Asparagus; Beetroot; Cabbage; Capsicum (pepper); Carrot; Cauliflower; Dwarf spinach; Eggplant (aubergine, brinjal); Endive; Horseradish (plant cuttings); Kohlrabi; Leek; Lettuce; Parsley; Parsnip; Peas; Radish; Sweet potato (plant tubers or cuttings); Swede turnip (swede); Swiss chard; Tomato; Turnip.

Western Cape: Winter rainfall areas

Asparagus; Beetroot; Broad bean; Capsicum (pepper); Carrot; Cucumber (under protection); Eggplant (aubergine, brinjal); Endive; Horseradish (plant cuttings); Kohlrabi; Leek; Lettuce (Cos); Onion; Parsnip; Peas; Radish; Spinach; Squash; Swiss chard; Tomato; Turnip; Vegetable marrow (all types).

Herbs

Brassica alba (mustard) and *Lepidium sativum* (cress) can be sown in all areas from August to May. Sow the seed in vermiculite in trays, either indoors or outdoors, in partial shade. Sow the cress first as it takes longer to mature than the mustard, then after three days sow the mustard. Start harvesting when the stems are about 10 to 12 cm tall. Use scissors to cut off as much as you need.

August – *a glorious month – the end of winter and the beginning of spring!*

88. Iris xiphium *are excellent as cut flowers.*

89. Veltheimia bracteata *are charming for the shadier parts of the spring garden.*

90. Lachenalia bulbifera *makes a charming pot plant.*

91. Leucojum vernum *(snowflake) is easy to grow and very rewarding.*

92. Rhododendron indicum, *the popular azalea.*

93. Scilla natalensis *is a charming indigenous plant.*

95. Ranunculus asiaticus *are among the most spectacular of the spring flowering bulbs.*

94. Narcissus *(daffodils): there are many varieties, and all are charming.*

96. Lampranthus deltoides *sparkles in the sunlight and makes a lovely splash of colour.*

SEPTEMBER

Officially it is summer, no matter what the thermometer says, and the danger of heavy frost has passed. Sowing summer flowering annuals now has priority. The willow trees know winter is over and are showing the first shimmer of green. The flowering plums and peaches add their pink, dark red and white blossoms to the beauty of the garden, and the scent of wisteria fills the air.

97. Kalanchoe tubiflora *has heads of pretty red flowers.*

98. Kalanchoe beharensis *(velvet leaf) has interesting foliage as well as attractive flowers.*

Annuals

Summer flowering annuals

If plants such as antirrhinums, hollyhocks and geraniums were attacked by rust last summer start preventive spraying now. Use Dithane, Funginex or a copper spray such as Copperchlor.

Prepare beds for sowing by digging in compost and 2:3:2 at the rate of 60 g per square metre.

All of these summer flowering annuals can be sown in all areas this month:

Acroclinium (Helipterum)
Ageratum houstonianum (floss flower)
Agrostemma githago milas (agrostemma)
Alcea rosea (hollyhock)
Alyssum
Amaranthus
Anchusa capensis 'Blue Bird'
Basil 'Dark Opal'
Bidens formosa (cosmos)
Callistephus chinensis (aster)
Campanula medium (Canterbury bells)
Celosia
Centaurea cyanus (cornflower)
Centaurea moschata (sweet sultan)
Chrysanthemum carinatum (annual variety)
Cleome hasslerana (spider flower)
Coleus
Convolvulus tricolor (morning glory)
Cotula turbinata
Dahlia (bedding)
Daucus carota var. carota (white lace flower or Queen Anne's lace)
Dianthus (pinks)
Didiscus (blue lace flower)
Eschscholtzia californica (Californian poppy) (sow in situ)
Euphorbia variegata (snow on the mountain) (soak seed before planting)
Gaillardia pulchella (blanket flower)
Gilia capitata
Gomphrena globosa (globe flower)
Gypsophila elegans (baby's breath)
Helianthus (sunflower)
Helichrysum (strawflower)
Impatiens balsamina (balsam)
Impatiens wallerana hybrids (busy Lizzy)
Kochia (Mexican fire bush)
Lavatera
Limonium bonduellii (statice or sea lavender)
Lobelia erinus (lobelia)
Lunaria annua (honesty)
Lupinus hartwegii (lupin)
Marigold
Matricaria maritima (feverfew)
Mimulus luteus (monkey flower)
Moluccella laevis (bells of Ireland)
Nicotiana
Nigella damascena (love-in-a-mist)
Papaver rhoeas (Shirley poppy)
Petunia
Portulaca
Reseda odorata (mignonette)
Rudbeckia hirta (gloriosa daisy)
Salpiglossis
Salvia splendens (scarlet salvia)
Scabiosa atropurpurea (pincushion flower)
Tropaeolum majus (nasturtium)
Verbena x *hybrida*
Zinnia

Winter flowering annuals

Pull these up as they finish flowering.

Perennials

If the plants were not given their spring treatment last month do this without delay. Tidy up all the clumps by removing the old leaves. Mulch with compost and apply 2:3:2 at the rate of 60 g per square metre, scattering this among the plants. Begin to water about once a week if the weather is dry, to encourage new growth.

Chrysanthemums: Water the plants and as soon as the new shoots are long enough start taking cuttings. Plant out rooted cuttings if large enough.

Delphiniums: Tidy up the clumps by removing the old leaves. Mulch and feed. Start watering regularly. Put out bait for slugs and snails. Take cuttings of new shoots. When the new shoots are 6 to 7 cm long scrape the soil away from the plant carefully and sever the cutting just below a node or leaf joint. Treat as a softwood cutting.

Paeonies: These can still be planted, or lifted and transplanted now. Give established plants a generous mulch of old, well-rotted manure. If this is not available apply a generous mulch of compost, plus about 2 tablespoons of 2:3:2 per plant. Start watering copiously at least once a week.

Lifting perennials: The perennials listed below can be lifted and divided now if this was not done in March. Water the plants well the day before they are to be lifted. The next day lift the clumps of plants with a fork, take them into the shade and cover with a damp sack to prevent the roots from drying. Small clumps are usually easy to divide and the roots can be teased apart with a hand fork, but it usually takes two people to divide large tough clumps. For these, use two forks placed back to back in the middle of the clump to force the roots apart. Some tough roots may have to be cut with a knife. For replanting choose young growths from the outer perimeter of the clumps. Discard the old woody portions.

Ajuga reptans (bugle mint)
Alyssum saxatile 'Gold Dust'
Anemone japonica (Japanese anemone)
Anthemis sancti-johannis
Arabis (rock cress)
Armeria maritima (thrift)
Aster novi-belgii (Michaelmas daisy)
Astilbe
Bergenia cordifolia
Begonia semperflorens (bedding begonia)
Campanula
Chrysanthemum 'Korean hybrids'
Chrysanthemum maximum (shasta daisy)

Dianthus (pinks)
Echinacea purpurea (pink rudbeckia)
Gaillardia x *grandiflora* (blanket flower)
Geum
Helleborus (hellebore)
Heuchera sanguinea (coral bells)
Liatris (gay feather)
Lobelia cardinalis
Lychnis chalcidonica (Jerusalem cross)
Macleaya cordata (plume poppy)
Monarda didyma (bee balm or bergamot)
Penstemon
Physostegia (obedient plant)
Platycodon grandiflorus (balloon flower)
Primula veris (primrose) (after flowering)
Primula x *polyantha* (polyanthus)
Pyrethrum roseum (painted daisy)
Salvia farinacea (blue salvia)
Salvia patens (dark blue salvia)
Scabiosa caucasica (pincushion flower)
Solidago (golden rod)
Stokesia laevis (Stoke's aster)
Verbena peruviana
Veronica (speedwell)
Viola odorata (sweet violet) (after flowering)

Water features

Now is the time to clean out fish ponds if this is necessary. Before cleaning out the fish pond catch the fish in a butterfly net (do not catch the fish by hand) and put them in a bath of water in a fairly shady place. Remove the water lilies and cover with wet sacks. Put other aquatic plants into the bath with the fish.

Drain the pond and remove the mud and debris, then scrub the sides with a wire brush (do not use soap or any chemicals). Rinse the pond and then refill with water.

To divide water lilies tear the roots apart, then, using a sharp knife, cut 15 cm of the growing tips off an old rhizome. Remove old brown roots and shorten the new white roots, then replant in a container filled with fresh soil.

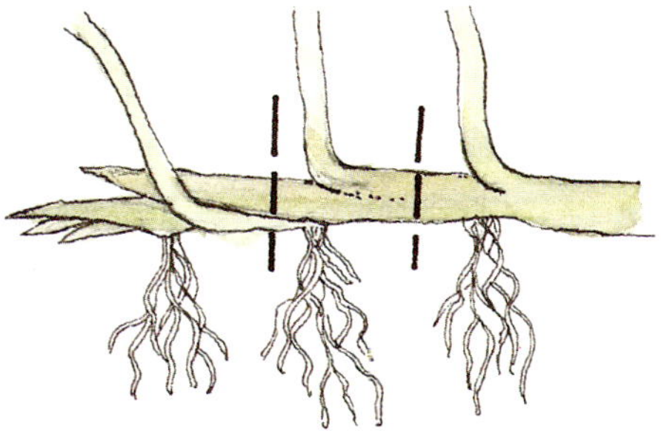

Put the newly potted water lilies back into the pond. Wait a day or two for the water to warm up before returning the other aquatic plants and the fish. Once again use a butterfly net to catch the fish.

Bulbs

Winter flowering bulbs

Continue to feed and water all bulbs which can be retained for replanting next season. These would include daffodils, narcissi, jonquils and the indigenous bulbs. Pull up anemones, ranunculus and tulips as their flowering season comes to an end. It is seldom worth keeping them from season to season.

Summer flowering bulbs

Any of the summer flowering bulbs listed below that were not planted last month can be planted now. After planting, water thoroughly, and then cover the bed with compost. In the weeks that follow water sparingly until the leaves appear.

Acidanthera bicolor
Albuca
Alpinia (shell flower)
Arum (see *Zantedeschia*)
Canna (Indian shot)
Chlidanthus fragrans (Peruvian daffodil)
Colocasia (elephant ear)
Crocosmia
Cyrtanthus macowanii (Ifafa lily)
Cyrtanthus purpurea (Vallota speciosa) (George or Knysna lily)
Dahlia (start into growth)
Dietes (*Moraea*)
Eucharis grandiflora (Amazon lily)
Eucomis (pineapple lily)
Galtonia candicans (Cape hyacinth or summer hyacinth)

100. Endymion hispanicus *(Spanish bluebell) is a charming spring flowering bulb.*

99. Arum palaestinum *(black arum) is an interesting and unusual plant.*

Gladiolus
Gloriosa superba (flame lily)
Habranthus
Haemanthus (see *Scadoxus*)
Hedychium (ginger lily)
Heliconia (lobster claw)
Hosta
Hymenocallis (spider lily)
Liatris (gay feather)
Liriope (turf lily)
Montbretia
Moraea (see *Dietes*)
Nerine bowdenii
Ornithogalum saundersiae (giant flowering chincherinchee)
Polianthes (tuberose)
Polygonatum (Solomon's seal)
Scadoxus (*Haemanthus*) (paint brush lily)
Scilla natalensis
Sprekelia (Maltese cross lily)
Tigridia pavonia (one day lily)
Tulbaghia
Zantedeschia albomaculata (yellow arum)
Zantedeschia pentlandii (deep yellow arum)
Zantedeschia rehmannii (small pink arum)
Zephyranthes (storm lily)

Cannas: If these were not given their spring treatment last month do this as soon as possible. Lift and replant if necessary. They are gross feeders and need rich, well-drained soil. If the rhizomes are not to be lifted, tidy up the bed, apply a dressing of 2:3:2 at the rate of 60 g per square metre, and cover with a generous mulch of compost. Water every two weeks until new growth starts.

101. Clivia miniata *is one of South Africa's most spectacular flowers.*

102. Tritonia *hybrid, invaluable in the garden as they flower later than the other spring bulbs.*

Dahlias: Plant before the shoots become too long or 'leggy'. Take cuttings when the new shoots are about 5 to 6 cm long. Cut the shoot off just below a node or leaf joint and treat as a softwood cutting.

Gladioli: Continue planting batches. Plants that have already come up should be sprayed once a week against thrips.

Taking softwood cuttings. 1. *Plants such as chrysanthemums, geraniums, delphiniums and lupins may be propagated by softwood cuttings. Select a shoot from the current year's growth, one that has not yet become hard or woody.* **2.** *Cut the shoot immediately below a leaf joint. Remove the lower leaves.* **3.** *Dip the cutting in a rooting hormone powder for softwood cuttings to ensure quicker rooting.* **4.** *Use a dibber to make a hole in prepared compost in a container. Insert the cutting almost up to the lower leaves.* **5.** *Gently firm in each cutting. Water well with a fine spray.*

Pot plants

Achimenes: Either remove a little of the top soil and replace with new, or completely repot if necessary. After doing this, water sparingly so that the plants do not rot before they have started rooting.

Amaryllis (Hippeastrums): Continue 'potting up' new bulbs. Feed those in bud and those in flower every two weeks with a liquid fertiliser such as Nitrosol, Multifeed P or Seagro fish emulsion. As the plants grow, water more frequently until they are being watered two or three times a week.

Cyclamen: When the leaves have died down water lightly from time to time so that the soil in the pots does not become bone dry.

Hyacinths, cinerarias, calceolarias, poinsettias and primulas: Continue to water all of these while they are in flower.

Potting and watering pot plants. *Never fill the pot with soil up to the brim but leave space for watering. Water round the rim of the pot. Never wet the leaves of hairy-leafed plants such as African violets or Rex begonias, and never water over the corms of cyclamen.*

Tuberous rooted begonias: Either remove a little of the top soil and replace with new, or completely repot if necessary. Pot up new tubers. Water sparingly after planting or repotting.

Sow seed of the following pot plants:

Begonia rex (painted leaf)
Begonia x *tuberhybrida* (tuberous rooted)
Capsicum (ornamental pepper)
Coleus
Impatiens wallerana (busy Lizzy)
Senecio cruentus (cineraria)
Sinningia speciosa (gloxinia)
Solanum capsicastrum (winter cherry)

Give all pot plants their spring treatment this month. From each pot carefully scratch off a little of the top soil, and replace with sifted compost.

Repot any plants that are pot bound. To discover whether or not a plant is pot bound, simply turn the pot upside down, and tap the rim lightly on the edge of a table. The soil ball should come out intact. The plant is pot bound if there is a mass of roots and very little soil visible.

Also repot any plants that have outgrown their pots or have become top heavy. Move them to pots just one size larger, unless you judge the plant to be too large even for that.

Lawns

Feed the grass once a month with 2:3:2 at the rate of 60 g per square metre. Scatter the fertiliser over the grass when it is dry and then water in immediately. Mow and water regularly during dry weather.

Shrubs

If the shrubs were not given a dressing of 2:3:2 and mulched with compost last month, do this now. Give small shrubs 1 tablespoon, and large shrubs 2 to 3 tablespoons of 2:3:2.

Softwood cuttings: Tip or softwood cuttings can be taken as soon as the new growth is long enough. Sever the cutting just below a leaf joint or node. Trim off the lower leaves, and dip the end of the cutting into a rooting hormone for softwood cuttings, such as Seradix No. 1. With a small dibber make a hole in a pan of moist rooting medium (sand, or two parts sand and one part peat). Insert the cutting making sure the base is resting on the sand, then firm in and water. Place the

Caring for your pot plants

Cleaning the foliage: Keep the leaves clean all through the year. Wipe large leaves with a soft damp cloth. Spray ferns and other delicate leaves with a fine spray. Dust hairy leaves (of plants such as African violets, gloxinias and Rex begonias) with a soft brush.

Watering: It is difficult to lay down hard and fast rules about how often to water. As a general guide, in summer keep the soil evenly moist (but never saturated). In winter water less frequently, but never allow the soil in the pots to dry out completely. Water ferns and orchids regularly all year round.

Never water over the corms or foliage of cyclamen, or over the foliage of hairy-leafed plants (such as African violets and Rex begonias). Always water these from the bottom.

Feeding: Either organic or inorganic fertilisers can be used for feeding pot plants. *Organic fertilisers* are suitable for delicate plants such as ferns and orchids. Two organic fertilisers are Nitrosol and Seagro fish emulsion. Although not a fertiliser Kelpak 66 liquid seaweed can also be used from time to time to stimulate growth.

Inorganic fertilisers include Baysol Plant Tonic; Lush Pot Plant Food; Multifeed P; Pokon and Vio-Bloom (for African violets).

Use these fertilisers at the rate recommended on the container, except where half strength is recommended below.

How often to feed pot plants

Most pot plants thrive if fed at regular intervals from September to April. But while some need to be fed once a week others may only need to be fed once a month. Follow the guidance given below, making a note of any exceptions.

Feed these once a week from September to April

Capsicum (ornamental peppers) (stop feeding once the fruit has formed)
Clivia miniata
Impatiens (both busy Lizzy and the New Guinea hybrid)
Sinningia speciosa (gloxinia) (when in flower)

Feed these every two weeks from September to April

Aglaonema (Chinese evergreen)
Anthurium (flamingo flower)
Aphelandra (zebra plant or saffron spike) (start feeding as soon as buds appear)
Asparagus plumosus (asparagus fern) (all types)
Begonia rex
Citrus mitis (calamondin orange)
Calathea zebrina (zebra plant)
Chamaedorea elegans (good luck palm or parlour palm) (at half strength)
Campanula isophylla (bell flower or star of Bethlehem)
Chlorophytum (spider plant)
Codiaeum (croton)
Columnea (lipstick plant, goldfish vine or Costa Rican plant)
Cordyline (New Zealand cabbage tree)
Crossandra
Dracaena (dragon tree)
Fatshedera (ivy tree)
Fatsia japonica (aralia)
Ficus benjamina (weeping fig)
Ficus elastica (rubber plant)
Ficus lyrata (fiddle back or fiddle leaf fig)
Fittonia (painted net leaf)
Hedera helix (ivy)
Howea forsteriana (Kentia palm or paradise palm)
Hypoestes phyllostachya (polka dot plant) (at half strength)
Maranta leuconeura (prayer plant) (at half strength)
Nephrolepis exaltata (sword or crested ladder fern) (at half strength)
Pelargonium (geranium)
Peperomia (at half strength)
Philodendron
Phoenix dactylifera (date palm)
Pilea cadierei (aluminium plant)
Pteris cretica (ribbon fern) (at half strength)
Schefflera (umbrella tree) (at half strength)
Solanum capsicastrum (winter cherry)
Spathiphyllum (snail plant)
Stephanotis floribunda (Madagascar jasmine) (at half strength)
Tradescantia fluminensis (wandering Jew)

Feed these every three weeks from September to April

Caladium (only start feeding in November)
Cocos nucifera (coconut palm) (at half strength)
Justicia brandegeana (Beloperone guttata) (shrimp plant)
Monstera deliciosa (delicious monster)
Pachystachys lutea (golden candles)
Saintpaulia ionantha (African violet)
Sansevieria trifasciata (mother-in-law's tongue)

Feed these once a month from September to April

Adiantum cuneatum (maidenhair fern) (at half strength)
Aspidistra lurida (aspidistra) (only the green variety)
Asplenium nidus (bird's nest fern) (at half strength)
Begonia x *tuberhybrida* (tuberous rooted) (when in flower in summer)
Dieffenbachia chelsoni (dumb cane)
Hoya carnosa (wax flower) (at half strength, from November to March)
Kalanchoe
Platycerium bifurcatum (staghorn fern) (at half strength)
Saxifraga stolonifera (mother of thousands) (at half strength)
Scindapsus aureus (devil's ivy or Joseph's coat) (at half strength, all year round)
Streptocarpus (Cape primrose) (at half strength)

103. Podalyria calyptrata *(sweet pea bush) has sweetly-scented, mauve-pink flowers set off by silver-grey foliage.*

pan in a semi-shaded warm place and keep the soil evenly damp.

Summer rainfall areas: Water all shrubs well every two weeks, paying special attention to those which will be flowering in the next few weeks.

Camellias: Give each bush 2 table-spoons (or more depending on size) of 2:3:2 and 60 g of magnesium sulphate (Epsom salts). Scatter this over the root area starting at least 10 cm away from the stem. Mulch under the plants with acid compost.

Fuchsias and other small shrubs: Pinch back new shoots to encourage bushy growth, and to shape.

Climbers

If the plants were not fed last month apply a dressing of 2:3:2 and mulch them with compost now.

Pinch back growing tips where bushy growth is needed. Train the plants on their supports.

Wisteria: If the plants were not pruned in July they can be pruned this month once they have finished flowering.

Summer rainfall areas: Water all climbers, except bougainvilleas, every two weeks.

Trees

Summer rainfall areas: Water all trees well at least once a month, paying special attention to flowering peaches, plums, cherries and crab apples. Keep the ground under all trees mulched with compost or bark.

104. Jasminum polyanthum *produces attractive pink buds which open out into clouds of sweetly-scented white flowers.*

105. Wisteria sinensis *is a beautiful, rampant, spring flowering climber.*

106. Alberta magna *is a magnificent sight when covered with bright red flowers.*

Fruit (and nuts)

Apples and pears: Start spraying against codling moth at three quarter petal drop i.e. when three quarters of the petals have dropped off the blossoms. Use Lebaycid (active ingredient: fenthion). Spray again after three weeks.

Bananas: Give each plant 30 g of 3:1:5 and 25 g of magnesium sulphate spread over the root area, starting 15 to 20 cm away from the stem. Keep the ground mulched with compost.

Cape gooseberries: Seed may still be sown in the summer rainfall areas.

Cherries: Water thoroughly once a week, letting the hose or sprinkler run for at least 30 minutes.

Citrus: When the trees are in flower water very well once a week.

Figs: Apply 100 g of 2:3:2 spread over the root area, starting at least 10 cm away from the trunk. Water regularly, especially in the summer rainfall areas.

Litchis: Continue to water well.

Mangoes: Continue to water very well once a month.

Pawpaws: Give each tree 450 g of superphosphate.

Raspberries: Feed with 3:1:5, scattering 25 g along a metre of row. Put down a generous mulch of compost, and water regularly especially in the summer rainfall areas.

Strawberries: Apply 3:1:5 at the rate of 60 g scattered along a metre of row, taking care not to get any on the leaves as it can burn them. Mulch between the rows with old, well-rotted manure, or with compost, and work it in lightly. Water well at least once a week.

Thinning out: Start thinning out apricots, peaches and plums when the fruit is the size of a large pea. (See illustration on page 84)

Vegetables

Continue routine care of all vegetables. Water every four or five days if the weather is dry. Feed every two weeks with a liquid fertiliser such as Nitrosol, Multifeed P, Lush or Seagro fish emulsion. Apply Kelpak 66 liquid seaweed once a month to stimulate growth and provide trace elements. Pull up the stumps of cabbages, cauliflowers, Brussels sprouts and broccoli.

Capsicum (peppers) and eggplant: Transplant seedlings as soon as they are about 10 to 15 cm high.

107. Prunus cerasifera *(flowering plum) is an ideal tree for a small garden.*

108. Prunus persica *'Clara Meyer' (flowering peach) is one of the most beautiful of the spring flowering trees.*

109. Prunus persica *'Carnation striped' (flowering peach) has unusual two-tone blossoms.*

110. Prunus persica *'Rubra plena' (flowering peach) has bright red flowers that contrast well with the white varieties of flowering peach*

Cucumber family: Use bait once a week, and after heavy rain, to protect the small fruits against pumpkin fly. Splash the bait onto the leaves in large drops.
Tomatoes: Spray against blight once a week from the time the seedlings come up. Use Dithane, Antracol or a copper spray such as Kopoxy or Copperchlor.

These vegetables can be sown in the various regions this month:

Transvaal and OFS Highveld

Asparagus; Beetroot; Broccoli; Cabbage; Capsicum (pepper); Carrot; Cucumber; Dwarf bean; Dwarf spinach; Eggplant (aubergine, brinjal); Globe artichoke (sow seed or plant suckers); Horseradish (plant cuttings); Jerusalem artichoke (plant tubers); Lettuce; Melon (all types); Parsley; Parsnip; Pumpkin; Radish; Runner bean; Swede turnip (swede); Swiss chard; Tomato; Vegetable marrow (all types).

Transvaal Middleveld

Asparagus; Beetroot; Broccoli; Cabbage; Capsicum (pepper); Carrot; Celery; Cucumber; Dwarf bean; Dwarf spinach; Eggplant (aubergine, brinjal); Globe artichoke (sow seed or plant suckers); Horseradish (plant cuttings); Jerusalem artichoke (plant tubers); Lettuce (Cos); Melon (all types); Parsley; Parsnip; Pumpkin; Radish; Runner bean; Swede turnip (swede); Swiss chard; Tomato; Turnip; Vegetable marrow (all types).

Transvaal Lowveld and warm frost-free areas

Capsicum (pepper); Dwarf bean; Eggplant (aubergine, brinjal); Globe artichoke (sow seed or plant suckers); Jerusalem artichoke (plant tubers); Parsley; Radish.

OFS and Northern Cape

Beetroot; Cabbage; Capsicum (pepper); Carrot; Cucumber; Dwarf bean; Dwarf spinach; Eggplant (aubergine, brinjal); Kohlrabi; Melon (all types); Peas; Parsley; Pumpkin; Radish; Runner bean; Swede turnip (swede); Swiss chard; Tomato; Turnip; Vegetable marrow (all types).

Natal Midlands

Cabbage; Capsicum (pepper); Carrot; Celery; Cucumber; Dwarf bean; Dwarf spinach; Eggplant (aubergine, brinjal); Globe artichoke (sow seed or plant suckers); Horseradish (plant cuttings); Jerusalem artichoke (plant tubers); Leek; Lettuce (Cos); Parsley; Parsnip; Pumpkin; Radish; Runner bean; Swede turnip (swede); Swiss chard; Tomato; Vegetable marrow (all types).

Eastern Cape and Karoo

Beetroot; Cabbage; Capsicum (pepper); Carrot; Cauliflower; Celeriac; Celery; Cucumber; Dwarf spinach; Eggplant (aubergine, brinjal); Endive; Kohlrabi; Leek; Lettuce; Melon (all types); Parsley; Parsnip; Radish; Sweet potato (plant tubers or cuttings); Swiss chard; Tomato; Vegetable marrow (all types).

Western Cape: Winter rainfall areas

Asparagus; Beetroot; Cabbage; Capsicum (pepper); Carrot; Celeriac; Cucumber (under protection); Dwarf bean; Eggplant (aubergine, brinjal); Leek; Lettuce (all types); Melon (all types); Onion; Parsley; Parsnip; Pumpkin; Radish; Runner bean; Spinach; Swiss chard; Squash; Tomato; Turnip; Vegetable marrow (all types).

111. Monarda didyma *'Cambridge Scarlet' (bergamot or bee balm) is an attractive garden plant.*

Herbs

This is the best month for sowing herbs, or for propagating them by layering or root division.

Annual herbs

**Anethum graveolens* (dill) (sow in situ in a sunny position)
**Anthriscus cerefolium* (chervil) (sow in situ in partial shade)
**Borago officinalis* (borage) (sow in situ in a sunny position)
***Brassica alba* (mustard) and *Lepidium sativum* (cress) (sow in partial shade)
**Carum carvi* (caraway) (sow in situ in a sunny position)
**Coriandrum sativum* (coriander) (sow in situ)
**Foeniculum vulgare* (fennel) (treat as an annual; sow in situ in a sunny position)
**Ocimum basilicum* (basil) (sow in situ)
**Pimpinella anisum* (anise) (sow in situ)
**Satureia hortensis* (summer savoury) (sow in situ in a sunny position)

Perennial herbs

Allium schoenoprasum (chives) (propagate by seed or root division)
Angelica archangelica (angelica) (a short-lived perennial; seed must be fresh)
**Artemesia dracunculus* (tarragon) (propagate from seed or root division)
Hyssopus officinalis (hyssop) (propagate by seed)
**Origanum onites* (marjoram) (propagate by seed or root division)
Melissa officinalis (balm) (propagate by root division)
Mentha piperita (peppermint) (propagate from runners)
Mentha pulegium (penny royal) (propagate from runners)
Mentha spicata (common mint) (propagate from runners)
**Rosmarinus officinalis* (rosemary) (propagate from seed)
**Rumex scutatus* (sorrel) (propagate from seed or root division)
Ruta graveolens (rue) (propagate from seed)
**Salvia officinalis* (sage) (propagate from seed)
**Thymus vulgaris* (thyme) (propagate from seed, layering or root division)

Note:
* Seed of these herbs is usually stocked by seedsmen or nurseries. The seed of herbs not commercially obtainable can however often be obtained from a fellow gardening enthusiast.
** Mustard and cress can be sown in all areas from August to May. Sow in vermiculite in trays, either indoors or outdoors, and in partial shade. Sow the cress first as it takes longer than the mustard to mature, then after three days sow the mustard. Start harvesting when the stems are about 10 to 12 cm tall. Use scissors to cut off as much as you need.

OCTOBER

This is the loveliest month in the garden. Roses are everywhere, set off by the deep blue of delphiniums and irises, and the tender green of trees. Those who sowed hardy summer flowering annuals late last summer will now have a fine display of snapdragons, dianthus, clarkias, early asters and Californian poppies.

Annuals

Summer flowering annuals

In the winter rainfall areas this is the main month for sowing summer flowering annuals. In other areas only quick maturing summer flowering annuals can still be sown. Those sown in August can be transplanted out into the garden.

Hardy summer flowering annuals

Some of the annuals sown in autumn should now be coming into flower, filling the gap between the last of the winter/spring flowering annuals and the first summer ones.

Perennials

Water all perennials if the weather is dry.

Chrysanthemums: Pinch back ('stop') the growing tips when the plants are about 10 cm tall, so that the plants will send out side shoots.

Delphiniums: Tie the flowering spikes to their stakes as they grow. Water the plants copiously, and protect from slugs and snails if necessary by putting out bait every evening.

Pelargoniums (geraniums): Pinch back ('stop') young plants to encourage side shoots.

Hellebores: Tidy up the plants by cutting off old flower heads and leaves.

Bulbs

Winter flowering bulbs

Continue watering and feeding winter flowering bulbs which have not yet died down. Feed every two weeks with a liquid fertiliser such as Multifeed P, Nitrosol or Lush.

Summer flowering bulbs

Although it is getting late in the season cannas and chlidanthus can still be planted. Continue planting gladioli.

As the summer flowering bulbs (planted in August and September) come up, increase the water supply to them, especially if the weather is dry.

Delphinium cuttings
1. *Favourite delphiniums can be propagated by cuttings. First lift the plant.* **2.** *Shake the excess soil from the roots so you can see what you are doing.* **3.** *Use a sharp knife held against the old stem and, cutting downwards, cut the shoot off cleanly.* **4.** *Note the good solid base on the cutting. Place the cutting in friable soil to which a little vermiculite has been added, firm in and water. Cuttings may be rooted in the open or in trays. Be careful not to over-water.*

112. Hemerocallis *(day lily) is a rewarding garden plant which flowers on and off throughout summer.*

Pot plants

See *SEPTEMBER 'Caring for your pot plants'*.

Continue feeding and watering primula obconica, polyanthus, primroses, poinsettias, daffodils, narcissi and hyacinths.
Amaryllis (Hippeastrums): Feed, and water every two to three days. Remove flowers as they fade, but leave the stems.
Achimenes and tuberous rooted begonias: Increase the water supply to these as they start growing.
Cyclamen: Water lightly occasionally to ensure that the soil does not dry out completely.
Cinerarias: Sow seed.

Lawns

Feed, water and mow regularly. If fungus attacks the grass treat the infected patches promptly before the infection spreads. Take control measures against caterpillars and crickets as soon as they are noticed. In the summer rainfall areas this is a good month to plant a new lawn.

Shrubs

Continue taking softwood cuttings.
Most shrubs need little special care at this time of the year, apart from a watering every two weeks during dry weather.
Fuchsias: Pinch back new growth to encourage side shoots. Start training to shape.
Camellias: In the middle of the month give each bush 30 g of ammonium sulphate. Dissolve this in 5 ℓ of water and apply as a liquid. Water before and after application.
Hydrangeas: Water twice a week and if the foliage is turning yellow give each bush a dressing of iron chelate at the rate recommended on the container, and 30 g of magnesium sulphate (Epsom salts). Dissolve both in 5 ℓ of water and apply to damp soil. Water in lightly.
Roses: Water at least once a week during dry weather. Remove faded flowers promptly. Start preventive spraying against black spot and mildew using any of the following remedies: Benlate (active ingredient: benomyl), Bayleton A (active ingredients: propineb/triadi-

113. Cuphea ignea *(cigarette bush) is an attractive and useful small shrub as it flowers all summer.*

114. Pentas lanceolata *is a colourful shrub for frost-free areas.*

115. Fuchsias *are versatile shrubs which can be grown in the garden, in containers or in hanging baskets.* **116.** Bougainvillea *toning well with the colours of the house.*

117. Mackaya bella *is an attractive shrub for a shady part of the garden.*

mefon), or Funginex (active ingredient: triforine). Spray once a week and after heavy rain, and add Kelpak 66 liquid seaweed, and Seagro fish emulsion or Nitrosol as a foliar feed, at the rates recommended on the containers.

To control the black and yellow fruit beetles that eat the blooms, spray with Karbaspray (active ingredient: carbaryl). To each 5 ℓ of spray add 10 ml of Lysol or Sanpic to give a longer lasting effect to the spray. This also helps to discourage the brown monkey beetle which burrows into the centre of the flowers.

Climbers

Water during dry weather. If it rains, make sure that plants on the lee of the house and garden walls are actually getting wet.

Trees

Water thoroughly about once a month during dry weather, and during rainy weather make sure that the rain water is actually penetrating the canopy of foliage. Keep the ground under the trees mulched with compost and/or bark.

Prune flowering apricots, peaches, plums and quinces if they need shaping and tidying up. Remove dead wood or damaged branches.

Fruit (and nuts)

Almonds: Give each tree 1 kg of 2:3:2 spread over the root area. Start at least 10 cm away from the trunk and go out to just beyond the drip line of the branches.

Apples, pears and quinces: Spray every three weeks against codling moth.

Apricots, peaches and plums: Finish thinning out the fruits before the pips get hard. Spray every 10 days against fruit fly. Use Lebaycid (active ingredient: fenthion) for both codling moth and fruit fly. Be sure to wait 10 days before picking the fruit. Ripcord can also be used for fruit fly and codling moth. Put out bait where spraying cannot be done because fruit is almost ready to pick.

1. *First thinning of pea-sized fruit.*

2. *Second thinning of marble-sized fruit.*

Thinning fruit

To ensure a crop of good sized apricots, nectarines, peaches and plums the fruit must be thinned out while still small. Do the thinning in two stages. Remove some when they are the size of a large pea, then thin again when the fruits are about the size of a marble. Leave one fruit to about every 10 cm of stem.

Fruit that ripens in October

Cherries: Black Biggereau; Black Tartarian; Early Rivers.
(Pick cherries when quite ripe as they do not ripen off the tree.)

Peaches: Alpha (October into November); Orion; Rhodes (Swellengrebel) (October into November).

Cape gooseberries: In the winter rainfall areas start sowing seed.

Citrus: Water well once every three weeks when the weather is dry. This is important at this time of the year.

Grape vines: If vines, especially young ones, are heavily laden, remove some of the bunches. This prevents the plant being weakened by producing too much fruit. If the bunches are too crowded thin out some of the berries using a pair of sharp pointed scissors.

Guavas: Prune the trees back quite hard. Apply 2 kg of 2:3:2 spread over the root area. Start at least 10 cm away from the trunk and go out to just beyond the drip line of the branches. Mulch generously with compost.

Litchis: Give each tree 500 g of 3:1:5 spread over the root area. Start at least 10 cm away from the trunk and go out to just beyond the drip line of the branches. Continue to water well.

Mangoes: Give each tree 2 kg of 3:1:5 spread over the root area.

Pecans: Give each tree 200 g of 2:3:2 spread over the root area. Start at least 10 cm away from the trunk and go out to just beyond the drip line of the branches. Water copiously during dry weather.

Raspberries: Water well at least once a week if the weather is dry.

Strawberries: Pick fruit as it ripens, and water at least once a week if the weather is dry.

Walnuts: Give each tree a 5 cm mulch of old, well-rotted manure, or compost with 150 g of 2:3:2 added. It is important to water thoroughly every three weeks. Mulch the ground with compost.

Vegetables

Water the vegetable garden every three to four days during dry weather and pull up weeds by hand.

Cucumber family: Splash bait on the foliage once a week and after heavy rain to protect the fruits from pumpkin fly.

October, *and the first flush of fragrant, colourful roses, the loveliest flowers of them all for many people.*

118. *Laura*

119. *Las Vegas*

120. *Summer Crest*

121. *Gold Glow*

122. Irises *and* roses *make good companions.*

123. *Charles Mallerin*

124. Bolusanthus speciosa *(Vanwyk's hout or wisteria tree), a beautiful indigenous tree.*

125. Jacaranda mimosifolia *is spectacular when in full flower.*

126, 127. Hymenosporum flavum *(Australian frangipani) is a quick-growing evergreen that bears fragrant yellow flowers in summer.*

Tomatoes: Spray against blight once a week and after heavy rain. Use Dithane, Kopoxy or Antracol.

These vegetables can be sown in the various regions this month:

Transvaal and OFS Highveld

Asparagus; Beetroot; Broccoli; Capsicum (pepper); Carrot; Celery; Cucumber; Dwarf bean; Dwarf spinach; Eggplant (aubergine, brinjal); Globe artichoke; Jerusalem artichoke (plant tubers); Lettuce (all types); Melon (all types); Parsley; Parsnip; Pumpkin; Radish; Runner bean; Swede turnip (swede); Sweet potato (plant tubers or cuttings); Swiss chard; Tomato; Vegetable marrow (all types).

Transvaal Middleveld

Asparagus; Beetroot; Broccoli; Capsicum (pepper); Carrot; Celery; Cucumber; Dwarf bean; Dwarf spinach; Eggplant (aubergine, brinjal); Globe artichoke; Jerusalem artichoke (plant tubers); Lettuce (Cos); Melon (all types); Parsley; Parsnip; Pumpkin; Radish; Runner bean; Swede turnip (swede); Sweet potato (plant tubers or cuttings); Swiss chard; Tomato; Vegetable marrow (all types).

Transvaal Lowveld and warm frost-free areas

Radish; Sweet potato (plant tubers or cuttings).

OFS and Northern Cape

Beetroot; Cabbage (early varieties); Capsicum (pepper); Carrot; Cucumber; Dwarf bean; Dwarf spinach; Eggplant (aubergine, brinjal); Kohlrabi; Lettuce; Melon (sweet and spanspek); Parsley; Pumpkin; Radish; Runner bean; Sweet potato (plant tubers or cuttings); Swede turnip (swede); Swiss chard; Tomato; Turnip; Vegetable marrow (all types).

Natal Midlands

Beetroot; Broccoli; Cabbage (early varieties); Capsicum (pepper); Carrot; Cucumber; Dwarf bean; Dwarf spinach; Eggplant (aubergine, brinjal); Leek; Lettuce (all types); Parsnip; Pumpkin; Radish; Runner bean; Sweet potato (plant tubers or cuttings); Swiss chard; Tomato.

Eastern Cape and Karoo

Beetroot; Carrot; Celeriac; Celery; Cucumber; Dwarf bean; Eggplant (aubergine, brinjal); Kohlrabi; Leek; Lettuce; Melon (all types); Parsley; Parsnip; Pumpkin; Radish; Runner bean; Sweet potato (plant tubers or cuttings); Tomato; Vegetable marrow (all types).

Western Cape: Winter rainfall areas

Beetroot; Cabbage; Carrot; Celery; Cucumber (under protection); Dwarf bean; Eggplant (aubergine, brinjal); Leek; Lettuce; Melon (all types); Onion; Parsley; Parsnip; Pumpkin; Radish; Runner bean; Spinach; Squash; Sweet potato (plant tubers or cuttings); Tomato; Turnip; Vegetable marrow (all types).

Herbs

These perennial herbs can be propagated from cuttings this month. Treat them as softwood cuttings.

Artemesia dracunculus (tarragon)
Hyssopus officinalis (hyssop)
Melissa officinalis (balm)
Mentha piperita (peppermint) (propagate from runners)
Mentha pulegium (penny royal) (propagate from runners)
Mentha spicata (common mint) (propagate from runners)
Origanum onites (marjoram)
Rosmarinus officinalis (rosemary)
Ruta graveolens (rue)
Salvia officinalis (sage)
Satureia montana (winter savoury)
Thymus vulgaris (thyme)

128. Cercis siliguastrum *(Judas tree) produces masses of rosy-purple flowers in early summer.*
129. Plumeria rubra *(frangipani): the red form of this popular shrub is striking.*

NOVEMBER

This month can be a bit of an anti-climax after the glamour of October unless gardeners planned ahead. Hardy summer flowering annuals sowed last autumn cheer this otherwise rather quiet period, and Oriental poppies in particular add a brilliant splash of colour. The flowering cherries provide a beautiful end to the blossom season.

Annuals

Summer flowering annuals

Water during dry weather. Feed every two weeks with a liquid fertiliser such as Seagro fish emulsion, Lush, Nitrosol or Multifeed P.
Remove faded flowers promptly. Stake where necessary. Watch for attack by red spider during hot dry weather. Put out bait for slugs and snails regularly in the late afternoon when the soil is wet after rain or watering.

The following quick growing summer flowering annuals can be sown now:

Alyssum
Dahlia (bedding)
Dwarf marigold
Eschscholtzia californica (Californian poppy)
Iberis umbellata (candytuft)
Impatiens balsamina (balsam)
Portulaca
Tagetes
Tropaeolum majus (nasturtium)

Winter flowering annuals

Sow seed of *Brassica oleracea* (ornamental kale), *Primula malacoides* (fairy primula), anemones and ranunculus. The last two can be treated as annuals as they can be raised from seed and if sown now will flower next winter.

130. Acanthus mollis *not only has handsome foliage but also produces spectacular flower spikes.*

Perennials

Give perennials the same care as described for summer flowering annuals.
Acanthus: After the plants have flowered, lift and divide if necessary.
Arctotis: Take softwood cuttings of young growths that are 6 to 7 cm long. Remove the lower leaves.
Chrysanthemums: Stake where necessary and feed every two weeks with a liquid fertiliser such as Nitrosol, Lush, Multifeed P or Seagro fish emulsion.
Delphiniums: Cut old flowering stems down to ground level. Give each plant 1 tablespoon of 2:3:2 scattered over the root area. Mulch with compost round the plants and water copiously during dry weather. Put out snail bait nearly every night to protect new growth from slugs and snails.
Sow seed of the following perennials. Best results are usually obtained from seed sown in seed trays.

Achillea millefolium (milfoil or yarrow)
Agathaea coelestis (Felicia amelloides) (blue daisy or blue marguerite)
Alcea rosea (hollyhock)
Alyssum saxatile 'Gold Dust'
Anchusa italica 'Dropmore' *(A. azura)* (bugloss)
Anthemis sancti-johannis
Aquilegia caerulea (columbine)
Arabis (rock cress)
Armeria maritima (thrift)
Aster novi-belgii (Michaelmas daisy)
Aster alpinus (Alpine aster)
Aubrieta (purple rock cress)
Bellis perennis (English daisy)
Bergenia cordifolia
Begonia (all types)
Centaurea candidissima (C. cineraria) (Dusty Miller)
Centaurea macrocephala
Cerastium tomentosum (snow in summer)
Chrysanthemum 'Korean' hybrids
Chrysanthemum maximum (Shasta daisy)
Delphinium 'Pacific Giant' and other hybrids (refrigerate seed)
Dianthus caryophyllus (carnation)
Dianthus deltoides (maiden pink)
Dianthus plumarius (cottage pink)
Digitalis (foxglove)
Doronicum cordatum (leopard's-bane)
Echinops ritro (violet thistle)
Gaillardia x *grandiflora* (blanket flower)
Gazania
Gerbera jamesonii (Barberton daisy)
Geum
Gypsophila paniculata (chalk plant)
Helianthemum (sun rose)
Heliotropium (heliotrope or cherry pie)
Heuchera sanguinea (coral bells)
Hibiscus moscheutos 'Southern Belle' (***keep in trays until spring)
Hypoestes sanguinolenta (polka dot plant)
Liatris (gay feather) (*sow in deep trays)
Limonium latifolia (fairy statice)
Limonium perezii (statice or sea lavender)
Limonium tataricum (statice or sea lavender)
Lobelia cardinalis
Lupinus 'Russel' hybrids (lupin) (soak seed and sow in individual pots)
Lupinus 'Minarette' hybrids (lupin)
Nepeta mussini (cat mint)
Nierembergia (cup flower)
Papaver orientale (Oriental poppy) (sow in situ; protect from snails)
Penstemon (beard tongue)
Phlox decussata (P. paniculata) (**refrigerate seed)
Platycodon grandiflora (balloon flower)
Primula x *polyantha* (polyanthus) (sold as *P. acaulis*)
Primula veris (primrose)
Scabiosa caucasia (scabious or pincushion flower)
Thalictrum (meadow rue) (***keep in trays until spring)
Viola odorata (sweet violet)

Note:
*Sow *Liatris* (gay feather) in trays that are about 10 cm deep. The plants can then be left in the trays when they die down, and the tubers can be planted out next spring when they are a bit bigger.
**Place the seed of *Phlox decussata* in an airtight container and put this in the refrigerator *(not the deepfreeze)* for four weeks before sowing, to break the dormancy.
****Thalictrum* (meadow rue) and *Hibiscus moscheutos* are deciduous and may be lost in winter if planted out when very small.

Bulbs

Winter flowering bulbs

As the foliage of the winter flowering bulbs dies down the bulbs can be lifted and dried in the shade. Remove old leaves and sand, then dust the bulbs with sulphur to prevent decay. Place in boxes in a cool dry place.

Summer flowering bulbs

Water at least once a week when the weather is hot and dry.
Agapanthus: Pay special attention to watering when the weather is dry.
Amaryllis family: Watch for attack by the amaryllis caterpillar or lily borer, and spray with Karbaspray (active ingredient: carbaryl) as soon as you notice them.
Cannas: Feed once during the month, scattering 1 tablespoon of 2:3:2 round each clump. Water well once a week.
Dahlias: Feed once during the month with a liquid fertiliser such as Nitrosol, Multifeed P or Seagro fish emulsion. Mulch the ground round the plants with compost. Water at least once a week, hosing down the foliage to discourage red spider. Tie plants to their

stakes as they grow, and start disbudding as soon as the buds are large enough.

Gladioli: Plant every four weeks for a succession of bloom. Plants that are already growing should be sprayed every week with Malathion, or have Aphid Granules scattered round them once a month to protect them from thrips and gladiolus fly.

Irises: As they finish flowering, lift and divide if the clumps have become crowded.

Liliums: Keep the ground round the plants well mulched with compost to ensure a cool root run. Feed once during the month with a liquid fertiliser such as Nitrosol, Multifeed P or Seagro fish emulsion. Water at least once a week if the weather is dry. Tie plants to stakes where necessary.

Scilla peruviana: Lift and divide if the plants have become overcrowded and the flowers are deteriorating.

131. Pelargonium x domesticum *(regal 'Geranium') has beautiful large flowers with attractive blotches.*

Lifting and storing bulbs
1. *Lift the bulbs. Avoid piercing the bulbs by inserting the fork well clear of the plant.* **2.** *Spread the bulbs out to dry in the shade.* **3.** *Remove any soil. Cut off the roots and shrivelled leaves.* **4.** *Store the bulbs in a box in a cool, dry shed.*

Pot plants

See *SEPTEMBER 'Caring for your pot plants'.*

As the weather gets warmer spray the foliage of anthuriums and other tropical plants to increase the humidity. In very dry areas place the plants on pebble trays to increase humidity.

To make a pebble tray put a layer of pebbles or chipped stone in a shallow dish or tray. Add just enough water to come below the surface of the pebbles. Stand the pot/s on the pebbles, ensuring that the base of the pot/s is *above* the water.

Amaryllis (Hippeastrums), achimenes and tuberous rooted begonias: Continue to feed and water these. Stake the begonias if the flower heads are becoming top heavy. Place a stake 15 to 20 cm long next to each plant and tie the stem to the stake with raffia or soft string. Be careful not to put the stakes through the tubers.

Caladiums: Start feeding every three weeks from now until April.

Cyclamen: Water lightly from time to time so that the soil does not become bone dry.

Daffodils, hyacinths and narcissi: If the foliage has died down do not water.

Sow seed of the following pot plants:

Calceolaria (from the middle of the month)
Cineraria (continue to sow to ensure a succession of flowers well into spring)
Primula malacoides (fairy primula)
Primula obconica
Primula x *polyantha* (polyanthus)
Primula veris (primrose)

Lawns

Feed the grass once a month with 2:3:2 at the rate of 60 g per square metre. Apply to dry grass and water in immediately. Mow regularly and water during very dry weather. Water in the morning. Treat fungus and pests if noticed.

Shrubs

Softwood cuttings can still be taken. Water during dry weather and keep the ground under the plants mulched with compost and/or bark.

Fuchsias: Continue pinching back the plants if still necessary. Feed once during the month with a liquid fertiliser such as Nitrosol, Lush, Multifeed P or Seagro fish emulsion. Water every two to three days.

Hydrangeas: Feed with hydrangea fertiliser at the rate given on the container, or give each bush 1 tablespoon of 2:3:2, and mulch with compost. Water at least twice a week during hot dry weather and hose down the foliage.

Prostanthera: Prune lightly and tidy up after the shrub has flowered. Remove straggly growth and any dead wood.

Pride of India: Water well during dry weather, and at the first sign of mildew spray with Benlate (active ingredient: benomyl) or Funginex (active ingredient: triforine).

Roses: Water once a week if the weather is dry. Remove faded flowers promptly. Spray once a week against black spot and mildew, and add foliar feed to the spray.

Watering shrubs. *Always water thoroughly. Make a dam of soil round the plant and water close to the base of the plant. Let the water trickle out slowly and fill the basin.*

Besides the fruit and monkey beetles mentioned last month the cockchafer beetle (also known as the brown or rose beetle) will also put in an appearance in many gardens this month. They eat holes in the leaves, and are active from now until about March.

Spraying with Karbaspray (as mentioned last month) will help to control all of these beetles. Catching the beetles at night by hand while they are feeding will also reduce their numbers considerably.

Climbers

Water during dry weather and keep the ground mulched with compost. In the summer rainfall areas make sure that the plants on the lee of the house and walls are actually getting wet when it rains.

Trees

If the weather is exceptionally dry water well once a month and keep the ground mulched with compost and/or bark.

Fruit (and nuts)

Continue spraying against fruit fly and codling moth. Put out bait regularly. (See the section *PESTS AND DISEASES* for details.)

Pick up all fallen fruit. Either soak it in water to which an insecticide has been added then bury it, or put it in a refuse bag, tie the bag up well, and dispose of it.

Bananas: Give each plant 30 g of 3:1:5 scattered over the root area, starting 15 to 20 cm away from the stem. Apply mulch, or renew the mulch if necessary.

Boysenberries and youngberries: Give the plants 60 g of 3:1:5 per metre of row. Water during dry weather.

Cape gooseberries: In the winter rainfall areas this is the best month for sowing seed.

Mulberries: Once all the fruit has been harvested give each tree 2 kg of 3:1:5 scattered over the root area. Start at least 10 cm away from the trunk and go out to just beyond the drip line of the branches. Mulch the ground with compost.

Fruit that ripens in November

Apricots: Alpha (at the end of November).
Berries: Boysenberries; Youngberries.
Cherries: Bing; Emperor Francis; Giant Heidelfinger; Governor Wood; Montmorency.
Mulberries
Peaches: ***White Freestone:*** Albatross; Alpha; Culemborg; Early Dawn; Killiekrankie (November into December); Rhodes (Swellengrebel). ***Yellow Freestone:*** Golden Amber; Ingwe; Sunray.
Plums: Beauty; Formosa (at the end of November); Methley (November into December).

Pecans and walnuts: Water copiously every two weeks during dry weather.

Raspberries: Mulch with old, well-rotted manure, or compost. If you use compost then add 60 g of 2:3:2 for every metre of row. Never let the plants lack water. Water well at least once a week during dry weather.

Vegetables

Water all vegetables regularly and feed once a month with a liquid fertiliser such as Nitrosol, Multifeed P or Lush. Splash bait on the leaves of all members of the cucumber family (cucumbers, marrows, melons, pumpkins) once a week and after heavy rain to protect the fruits from pumpkin fly.

Spray tomatoes once a week against blight and tie the plants to their stakes as they grow, using raffia or soft string.

Pick beans two or even three times a week to encourage the plants to go on bearing. Plant small batches of dwarf beans about once a month for succession. Do not pick beans when the plants are wet. The leaves are more

132. Calodendron capense *(Cape chestnut) is a beautiful flowering tree.*

133. Callistemon viminalis *(weeping bottlebrush) has graceful drooping branches.*

likely to be attacked by fungi if handled when wet.

These vegetables can be sown in the various regions this month:

Transvaal and OFS Highveld

Broccoli; Brussels sprouts; Cabbage (main sowing); Cauliflower (early varieties); Celeriac; Celery; Cucumber; Dwarf bean; Dwarf spinach; Globe artichoke; Jerusalem artichoke (plant tubers); Kohlrabi; Leek; Melon (all types); Pumpkin; Runner bean; Sweet potato (plant tubers or cuttings); Tomato; Vegetable marrow (all types).

Transvaal Middleveld

Broccoli; Cabbage (main sowing); Cauliflower (main sowing); Celery; Cucumber; Dwarf bean; Dwarf spinach; Globe artichoke; Jerusalem artichoke (plant tubers); Kohlrabi; Leek; Lettuce (Cos); Melon (all types); Pumpkin; Radish; Runner bean; Sweet potato (plant tubers or cuttings); Tomato; Vegetable marrow (all types).

Transvaal Lowveld and warm frost-free areas

Sweet potato (plant tubers or cuttings).

OFS and Northern Cape

Beetroot; Broccoli; Brussels sprouts; Cabbage (main sowing); Carrot; Cauliflower (main sowing); Dwarf bean; Dwarf spinach; Kohlrabi; Lettuce; Parsley; Pumpkin; Radish; Runner bean; Swede turnip (swede); Sweet potato (plant tubers or cuttings); Swiss chard; Tomato; Turnip; Vegetable marrow (all types).

Natal Midlands

Broccoli; Brussels sprouts; Cabbage (main sowing); Dwarf bean; Dwarf spinach; Lettuce; Pumpkin; Runner bean; Sweet potato (plant tubers or cuttings); Tomato.

Eastern Cape and Karoo

Beetroot; Broccoli; Brussels sprouts; Cabbage (main sowing); Carrot; Cauliflower (main sowing); Cucumber; Dwarf bean; Lettuce; Parsley; Pumpkin; Radish; Runner bean; Sweet potato (plant tubers or cuttings); Swiss chard; Vegetable marrow (all types).

Western Cape: Winter rainfall areas

Beetroot; Cabbage (main sowing); Carrot; Cauliflower (early varieties); Cucumber; Dwarf bean; Lettuce; Melon (sweet and spanspek); Parsley; Pumpkin; Radish; Runner bean; Spinach; Squash; Sweet potato (plant tubers or cuttings); Turnip; Vegetable marrow (all types).

Herbs

Chervil: Keep plants from flowering by pinching the buds as they appear.
Mustard and cress: These can be sown in all areas from August to May. Sow the cress three days before sowing the mustard so that both will mature at the same time. Start harvesting when the stems are about 10 to 12 cm tall. Use scissors to cut off as much as you need.

DECEMBER

There is much to enjoy in the garden again. The second flush of roses and the early summer flowering annuals are just beginning to open, promising a beautiful summer garden again. Christmas hydrangeas, liliums and day lilies add their enchantment to the garden.

Annuals

Summer flowering annuals

Continue watering during dry weather. Feed twice a month with a liquid fertiliser such as Nitrosol, Multifeed P, Lush or Seagro fish emulsion. Remove faded flowers promptly. Watch for red spider and put out bait for slugs and snails.

The following quick growing summer flowering annuals can still be sown:

Alyssum
Dahlia (bedding)
Dwarf marigold
Eschscholtzia californica (Californian poppy)
Iberis umbellata (candytuft)
Impatiens balsamina (balsam)
Portulaca
Tagetes
Tropaeolum majus (nasturtium)

Winter flowering annuals

Brassica oleracea (ornamental kale) and *Primula malacoides* (fairy primula) can still be sown this month.

Perennials

Any of these perennials that were not sown last month can still be sown now:

Achillea millefolium (milfoil or yarrow)
Agathaea coelestis (Felicia amelloides) (blue daisy or blue marguerite)
Alcea rosea (hollyhock)
Alyssum saxatile 'Gold Dust'
Anchusa italica 'Dropmore' *(A. azura)* (bugloss)
Anthemis sancti-johannis
Aquilegia caerulea (columbine)
Arabis (rock cress)
Armeria maritima (thrift)
Aster novi-belgii (Michaelmas daisy)
Aster alpinus (Alpine aster)
Aubrieta (purple rock cress)
Bellis perennis (English daisy)
Bergenia cordifolia
Begonia (all types)
Centaurea candidissima (C. cineraria) (Dusty Miller)
Centaurea macrocephala
Cerastium tomentosum (snow in summer)
Chrysanthemum 'Korean' hybrids
Chrysanthemum maximum (Shasta daisy)
Delphinium 'Pacific Giant' and other hybrids (refrigerate seed)
Dianthus caryophyllus (carnation)
Dianthus deltoides (maiden pink)
Dianthus plumarius (cottage pink)
Digitalis (foxglove)
Doronicum cordatum (leopard's-bane)
Echinops ritro (violet thistle)
Gaillardia x *grandiflora* (blanket flower)
Gazania
Gerbera jamesonii (Barberton daisy)
Geum
Gypsophila paniculata (chalk plant)
Helianthemum (sun rose)
Heliotropium (Heliotrope or cherry pie)
Heuchera sanguinea (coral bells)
Hibiscus moscheutos 'Southern Belle' (***keep in trays until spring)
Hypoestes sanguinolenta (polka dot plant)
Liatris (gay feather) (*sow in deep trays)
Limonium latifolia (fairy statice)
Limonium perezii (statice or sea lavender)
Limonium tataricum (statice or sea lavender)
Lobelia cardinalis
Lupinus 'Russel' hybrids (lupin) (soak seed and sow in individual pots)
Lupinus 'Minarette' hybrids (lupin)
Nepeta mussini (cat mint)
Nierembergia (cup flower)
Papaver orientale (Oriental poppy) (sow in situ; protect from snails)
Penstemon (beard tongue)
Phlox decussata (P. paniculata) (**refrigerate seed)
Platycodon grandiflorus (balloon flower)
Primul x *polyantha* (polyanthus) (sold as *P. acaulis*)
Primula veris (primrose)
Scabiosa caucasia (scabious or pincushion flower)
Thalictrum (meadow rue) (***keep in trays until spring)
Viola odorata (sweet violet)

Note:
*Sow *Liatris* (gay feather) in trays that are about 10 cm deep. The plants can then be left in the trays when they die down, and the tubers can be planted out next spring when they are a bit bigger.
**Place the seed of *Phlox decussata* in an airtight container and put this in the refrigerator *(not the deepfreeze)* for four weeks before sowing, to break the dormancy.
****Thalictrum* (meadow rue) and *Hibiscus moscheutos* are deciduous and may be lost in winter if planted out when very small.

Acanthus: Lift and divide if necessary. Cut down old leaves and flower stems to ground level. Give each clump 60 g of 2:3:2, spreading this round the clump. Mulch with compost. Water once a week during dry weather.
Delphiniums: Water thoroughly every two or three days during dry weather. Feed every two weeks with a liquid fertiliser such as Nitrosol, Lush, Multifeed P or Seagro fish emulsion.

Refrigerate the seed of 'Pacific Giant' delphiniums for sowing in January.

Bulbs

Agapanthus: Water thoroughly at least once a week during dry weather.
Amaryllis belladonna (March lily): In the summer rainfall areas lift and replant if necessary.

134. Lilium lancifolium *(L. tigrinum), a 'must' for the summer garden.*

Amaryllis family: Watch for attack by the amaryllis caterpillar or lily borer and spray with Karbaspray as soon as you notice this pest.
Gladioli: Continue planting for succession. Spray against thrips and gladiolus fly.
Irises: After the plants have finished flowering, lift and divide if the rhizomes have become overcrowded.
Nerine sarniensis (Guernsey lily): These bulbs can be planted this month.

135. Iris xiphium

136. Hydrangea macrophylla *'Regular' (white hydrangea) has a special charm.*

137. Aristolochia gigantea *is a rampant climber with most unusual flowers.*

139. Hydrangea macrophylla *bearing true blue flowers such as this are much prized.*

138. Thunbergia alata *(black-eyed Susan) is a charming climber.*

140. Thunbergia grandiflora *is a rampant climber with lovely clear blue flowers.*

Pot plants

See *SEPTEMBER 'Caring for your pot plants'.*

Amaryllis (Hippeastrums): Continue feeding every two weeks with a liquid fertiliser such as Seagro fish emulsion, Nitrosol or Multifeed P to build up the bulbs for next season.

Achimenes and tuberous rooted begonias: Feed every two weeks with a liquid fertiliser such as Seagro fish emulsion, Nitrosol or Multifeed P. Water regularly. Stake begonia flower heads if necessary.

Sow the following seeds. Best results are usually obtained from seed sown in trays:

Calceolaria
Cineraria (from the middle of the month)
Primula malacoides (fairy primula)
Primula obconica
Primula x *polyantha* (polyanthus)
Primula veris (primrose)

Lawns

Feed once a month with 2:3:2 at the rate of 60 g per square metre. Water every two weeks during dry weather. Mow fine grass once a week and kikuyu twice a week. Watch for attack by fungus and insects, and treat promptly if noticed.

Shrubs

Water every two weeks during dry weather and mulch the ground with compost.

Camellias: Give each bush 30 g of magnesium sulphate (Epsom salts). Dissolve this in 5 ℓ of water and apply as a liquid. Mulch or renew the mulch if necessary, and water once a week during dry weather.

Climbers

Water every two weeks during dry weather, and keep the ground mulched with compost. Tie climbers to their supports regularly.

Clerodendrum thomsoniae (bleeding heart): Remove the faded flower heads, cutting down to first node or leaf joint.

Doxantha unguis-cati (cat's claw creeper): Thin out quite hard and remove seed pods, not only because they are untidy, but also because in some areas the plant is becoming a weed as a result of its prolific seeding.

Trees

Water once a month if the weather is hot and dry.

Mulching shrubs and trees. *Spread a layer of mulch over the root area of trees and shrubs. The mulch helps the soil retain moisture in dry weather, it discourages weeds, and it protects the roots from frost.*

Fruit (and nuts)

Continue to spray against fruit fly and codling moth, being very careful to observe the safety period. Put out bait regularly. (See the section *PESTS AND DISEASES* for details.)

Boysenberries, raspberries and youngberries: When these have finished bearing cut the old fruiting canes down to ground level. Tie the new canes on to the supports to take the place of those cut down.

Cape gooseberries: Finish sowing seed in the winter rainfall areas.

Citrus: Give each tree 2 kg of 3:1:5 spread over the root area, starting at least 10 cm away from the trunk and going out to just beyond the drip line of the branches. Water well every three weeks during dry weather.

Litchis: Give each tree 500 g of 3:1:5 spread over the root area, starting at least 10 cm away from the trunk and going out to just beyond the drip line of the branches.

Fruit that ripens in December

Apricots: Bulida (early December); Early Cape (early December); Peeka (late December); Piet Cillie (mid December); Royal (late December).

Grapes: Agawani (December into January); Queen of the Vineyard (December into January).

Peaches: ***White Freestone:*** Babcock; Boland; C. O. Smith; Duke of York; Killiekrankie; Van Riebeeck. ***Yellow Freestone:*** Clocolan; Ficksburg; Jubilee; Safari; Saturn. ***Yellow Clingstone:*** Oom Sarel; Professor Izak Malherbe.

Pears: December Pear (December into January).

Plums: Eclipse; Elephant Heart; Flaming Delicious; Santa Rosa (December into January).

Vegetables

Water at least once a week if the weather is hot and dry. Feed from time to time with a liquid fertiliser such as Multifeed P, Nitrosol, Lush or Seagro fish emulsion. Pull up weeds by hand, and mulch the ground between the rows with compost.

Pick beans two or three times a week and sow small batches of seed about once a month for succession. Splash bait on the leaves of all members of the cucumber family (cucumbers, marrows, melons, pumpkins) to protect the fruit from pumpkin fly.

Spray tomatoes against blight once a week and after heavy rain.

These vegetables can be sown in the various regions this month:

Transvaal and OFS Highveld

Broccoli; Brussels sprouts; Cauliflower (main sowing); Cabbage (main sowing); Celeriac; Celery; Cucumber; Dwarf bean; Globe artichoke; Jerusalem artichoke (plant tubers); Kohlrabi; Leek; Lettuce (Cos); Runner bean; Sweet potato (plant tubers or cuttings); Vegetable marrow (bush types only).

Transvaal Middleveld

Broccoli; Cabbage (main sowing); Cauliflower (main sowing); Celeriac; Celery; Cucumber; Dwarf bean; Dwarf spinach; Globe artichoke; Jerusalem artichoke; Kohlrabi; Leek; Lettuce (Cos); Runner bean; Sweet potato (plant tubers or cuttings); Tomato; Vegetable marrow (all types).

Transvaal Lowveld and warm frost-free areas

Capsicum (pepper); Celeriac; Sweet potato (plant tubers or cuttings).

OFS and Northern Cape

Beetroot; Broccoli; Brussels sprouts; Cabbage (main sowing); Carrot; Cauliflower (main sowing); Celeriac; Celery; Dwarf bean; Dwarf spinach; Kohlrabi; Lettuce; Parsley; Pumpkin; Radish; Runner bean; Swede turnip (swede); Sweet potato (plant tubers or cuttings); Swiss chard; Turnip.

Natal Midlands

Beetroot; Broccoli; Brussels sprouts; Cabbage (main sowing); Cauliflower (early varieties); Celeriac; Dwarf bean; Lettuce (Cos); Parsley; Runner bean; Sweet potato (plant tubers or cuttings).

Eastern Cape and Karoo

Beetroot; Broccoli; Brussels sprouts; Cabbage (main sowing); Carrot; Cauliflower (main sowing); Cucumber; Dwarf bean; Kohlrabi; Lettuce; Parsley; Runner bean; Sweet potato (plant tubers or cuttings); Vegetable marrow (all types).

Western Cape: Winter rainfall areas

Broccoli; Brussels sprouts; Cabbage (main sowing); Cauliflower (main sowing); Dwarf bean; Lettuce; Runner bean; Vegetable marrow (all types).

Herbs

Chervil: Keep plants from flowering by pinching the buds as they appear.

Mustard and cress: These can be sown in all areas from August to May. Sow the cress three days before sowing the mustard so that both will mature at the same time. Start harvesting when the stems are about 10 to 12 cm tall. Use scissors to cut off as much as you need.

141. Digitalis purpurea *(foxgloves) are striking, shade-loving plants.*

Making your garden grow

As with all living things, plants need food to grow vigorously. This they must be able to take up from the soil in the form of minerals. These can be applied to your garden by way of the range of patent inorganic fertilisers available from most nurseries, garden shops and supermarkets. But minerals alone are not enough and organic material in the form of compost and manure must also be added to the soil on a regular basis.

Not only does organic matter improve the tilth or crumb structure and water holding capacity of the soil but it also provides a breeding ground for teeming hordes of minute organisms belonging to both the vegetable and animal kingdoms. Many of these organisms convert fresh organic matter into humus (compost) and, in doing so, release plant nutrients in organic forms which can be taken up by the plants.

Animal manures are a valuable source of plant nutrients and organic matter, but as manures are nowadays rather scarce and expensive, gardeners have to rely on compost and fertilisers. The compost keeps their soil friable and provides a hospitable environment for the micro-organisms. The fertilisers provide a steady supply of essential nutrients. Every scrap of waste plant material from the garden and kitchen should be converted into compost, and either dug in when preparing beds or used as a mulch. The value of mulching cannot be too strongly emphasised.

Fertilisers

Inorganic fertilisers

For healthy growth plants need nitrogen (N), phosphorus (P) and potassium (K). These three are known as the major elements, or the 'Big Three'. The fertilisers are always mixed in the above order and the figures 2:3:2 or 3:1:5, for example, on the bags represent the ratio of NPK. The number in brackets after these figures, for example, (14) after 2:3:2, gives the percentage of active ingredients. The higher the figure the stronger the mixture, the balance being made up of an inert filler.

Nitrogen (N): This is a constituent of every living cell and is required by plants in large amounts. It promotes vegetative growth, large dark green leaves and bulk, and is specially important for leaf crops such as cabbage and spinach. It can be applied in the form of ammonium sulphate which has an acid reaction, or limestone ammonium nitrate (LAN) which is neutral.

Deficiency signs: Light green to yellow lower leaves and slow, stunted growth.

Excess: Weak stems, rank growth and soft tissues which are subject to damage by cold and fungus diseases such as mildew. The plants may not mature properly and often produce few flowers.

Phosphorus (P): This promotes and hastens the formation of flowers and fruits. It helps plants to take up nitrogen and potassium and increases resistance to disease. Phosphorus can be applied as superphosphate. As most South African soils are deficient in phosphorus it should be applied when preparing for all crops and especially for fruit trees, grape vines and berries. Place it well down in the soil where it will be readily available to the roots, which it will not burn.

Deficiency signs: Plants such as hydrangeas fail to make flower buds, growth is slow and root development is poor, as is the setting of flowers and fruits. Leaves often have a bronze tinge.

Excess: There is seldom an excess of phosphorus in the soil.

Potassium (K): This plays a part in sugar and starch production in plants and is important for crops which

A diagram illustrating the functions of a plant which allow it to absorb moisture and nutrition from the soil and draw moisture and energy from the air, ridding itself of excess chemicals by a process of transpiration.

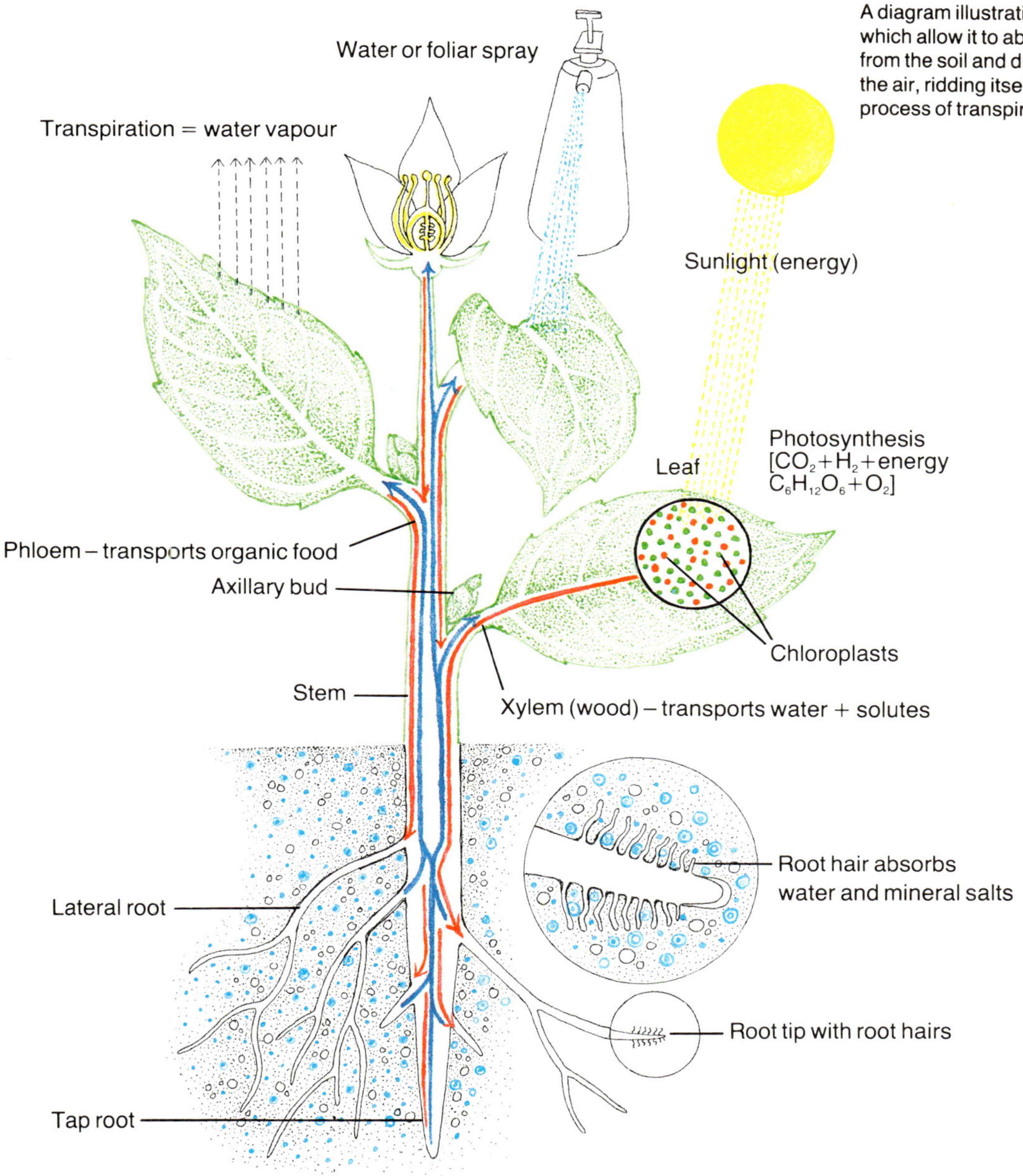

manufacture large quantities of these, namely tomatoes, apples, strawberries and other fruits, as well as potatoes and root crops. Potassium also helps to strengthen stems. It can be applied as potassium sulphate or potassium nitrate.

Deficiency signs: Leaf tips and margins turn light brown. This discoloration gradually progresses towards the centre and between the veins until finally the leaves curl up, go completely brown and fall off. Fruit, potatoes and root crops are of poor quality.

Excess: This causes hard, very stocky growth.

Magnesium sulphate (Epsom salts): This is as important as the 'Big Three' as it is an essential element of chlorophyll, the green colouring matter in leaves. Dolomitic lime and animal manures are sources of magnesium sulphate. However, as it is not advisable to apply lime to the soil indiscriminately, and as animal manures are scarce, gardeners can apply a light dressing of magnesium sulphate (Epsom salts) each spring with benefit.

Deficiency signs: These show in the older leaves first. These develop discoloured areas and dead tissue between the veins. A serious deficiency can result in growth ceasing.

Excess: An excess of magnesium sulphate is unlikely to harm plants, but an overdose of dolomitic lime will alter the pH of the soil and this in turn can adversely affect plants.

Nitrogen, phosphorous and potassium
Plants must have a balanced diet as the fertilisers interact with each other, and an excess can be as harmful as a deficiency. With this in mind the following mixtures have been formulated:

- 2:3:2 (a good all round mixture for flowers, vegetables and lawns)
- 3:1:5 (with extra potassium; useful for potatoes and other root crops, strawberries, tomatoes, fruit trees and sweet peas; applied in early autumn it will also harden up the new growth of roses and make them more resistant to cold)
- 4:1:1 (useful for plants grown for their foliage)

Calcium: This is also a constituent of plant cells, occurring in the greatest amount in the leaves. It plays a part in cementing cell walls together and stiffening stems, it improves the properties and physical condition of the soil, the availability of nutrients and the activity of soil micro-organisms. However, its most important role concerns the pH of the soil (see box). Calcium can be applied in the form of agricultural lime. Dolomitic limestone (which contains large amounts of magnesium) may also be used.

Deficiency signs: Soils lacking in calcium are likely to be too acid and this will inhibit the growth of all but acid-loving plants such as azaleas, camellias, ericas and proteas.

Excess: Too much lime will raise the pH of the soil so it is important that lime always be applied with great circumspection.

Sulphur: There is little need for gardeners to worry about a shortage of sulphur as nearly all the fertilisers are supplied in sulphate form, for example, ammonium sulphate, potassium sulphate.

Trace elements: Boron, copper, iron, manganese and molybdenum are only needed in minute quantities, but they play a vital role in plant nutrition. They can be applied as trace-element mixtures according to the directions on the container, or in the form of seaweed meal when preparing the soil for planting, or as liquid seaweed in the form of a drench or foliar feed.

The pH of the soil

pH is chemistry shorthand for 'potential hydrogen' and refers to the level of acidity or alkalinity of any substance, including soil. It is of vital consideration in the garden because if the pH balance is incorrect for a plant, either too acid or too alkaline, then that plant will just never flourish, and will probably die.

The pH scale indicates this acidity or alkalinity and ranges from 0 to 14, with 7 being neutral. The lower the figure the more acid the soil and the higher the figure the more alkaline the soil. You can test your own soil fairly accurately with a soil testing kit or instrument available from any garden shop or nursery, but it is important to follow the instructions carefully to avoid the possibility of ending up with misleading results.

Calcium is most important in achieving the correct pH balance as soils deficient in this chemical are likely to be very acid. Soils deficient in calcium are usually found in high rainfall areas, but in South Africa these are few and far between. As it is much easier to make acid soils alkaline than alkaline soils acid, calcium in the form of agricultural or dolomitic lime should be applied with great circumspection, and then only once every three to four years.

It is difficult to bring the pH of the soil down. Finely ground sulphur can be applied but this takes several months to be effective. It is best to apply this in spring. If the pH has not been reduced within a reasonable time, more sulphur can be applied. When preparing holes for acid-loving shrubs, sprinkle sulphur on the sides of the holes and mix a little with the soil, together with plenty of peat (preferably imported) and acid compost (made from pine needles, oak, wattle and tea leaves).

Most garden plants can be grown successfully in soil with a pH of 6,5 to 7 but there are some, known as calcifuges, which dislike lime in the soil. These include most of the Cape and Australian hardwood plants, members of the erica family (ericas, rhododendrons, azaleas), members of the protea family, gardenias, hydrangeas, and beardless irises. Calciphilous plants, on the other hand, are lime loving and include stocks, sweet peas, bearded irises, gazanias, Namaqualand daisies and members of the ranunculus family.

If, when preparing beds, lime and manure or compost are to be added, give the dressing of lime a month before the manure or compost. The contact of lime with such nitrogenous fertilisers leads to the liberation of ammonia into the air and they should, therefore, never be applied together. Lime should be applied to the surface of the soil and lightly raked in.

Applying fertiliser

When applying fertilisers it is better to use small quantities at regular intervals, rather than large quantities less frequently.

Spread the fertiliser out evenly over the soil and try to avoid getting it on foliage as some can burn. When fertilising trees, especially fruit trees and shrubs, never pile the fertiliser against the trunk or stem, but start at least 10 cm away from the stem and preferably about 20 cm away, and spread it out to just beyond the drip line of the branches. Always apply to damp soil and water in immediately after application.

Organic fertilisers

The most important function of bulky organic manures is to supply humus to the soil, but they also provide plant nutrients and act as a useful supplement to inorganic fertilisers.

Compost: Animal manures are a scarce and expensive luxury today and most of us have to rely on compost as the best substitute. Well-made compost can contain 2-2,5% N: 0,5-1,0% P: 0,5-2,0% K, which compares quite favourably with farmyard manure.

Leaf mould (or leaf soil): This is made up of leaves which have decomposed. It can be made by alternating 15 cm layers of damp leaves with thin layers (2,5 to 5 cm) of soil in small heaps. Anything up to a year is required for the material to break down, and the end product is excellent for pot plants, especially ferns. Leaves from trees growing on alkaline soil will provide an alkaline leaf mould.

Manures: Farmyard manure may be that of horses, cows, pigs, sheep or poultry (including pigeons). The average analysis of these is as follows, in kg per metric ton:

	N	P	K
Cow	4,9	1,3	4,5
Horse	5,9	1,8	4,5
Pig	4,9	2,7	4,0
Poultry	9,4	8,0	4,5
Sheep	9,0	6,2	3,6

If manure cannot be dug into the ground immediately it should be stored in a heap, covered with a little soil and kept damp. Care must always be taken when manuring ground before planting or when using manure as a mulch to ensure that it has broken down fairly well. Fresh manure burns. Old, well-rotted manure, which has neither heat nor smell, will not harm plants and it can be dug in just prior to planting.

Cow manure: This is useful on light, sandy soils. It can be used as an activator when making compost, and for making liquid manure.

Green manuring: Soil, especially light sandy soil, can be improved by a 'green manure'. This is a cover crop that is grown and dug in while still green. Legumes such as lupins, cow peas and sun hemp, with their deep rooting systems and ability to fix atmospheric nitrogen, are particularly valuable for this purpose. Italian ryegrass can also be used, but after it has been turned in, a dressing of ammonium sulphate at the rate of 15 to 30 g per square metre should be applied. This supplies the extra nitrogen necessary for the decomposition of the material and helps to hasten the process.

the colour of weak tea before applying to plants. It is advisable to keep a lid on the drum as the manure does not smell pleasant.

Pig manure: This has a strong, offensive odour, is 'cold' and, although it does not accelerate the breakdown of vegetable matter on the compost heap to any extent, it does produce good compost if one is prepared to wait for it.

Poultry manure: This, being concentrated, should be used with care. It is best used dried and pulverised, applied at the rate of 100 g per square metre and lightly raked into the soil. It makes excellent compost and liquid manure.

Sheep manure: As can be seen from the analysis, this is rich in nutrients. In southern Africa, great care should be taken to ensure that the manure does not come from brackish areas. The salts in brackish manure can be detrimental to some crops.

Sowing green manure crops

Cow peas
- Winter rainfall areas – August/September
- Natal – from November to January
- Transvaal and OFS – from October to December

Italian ryegrass
- from March to June

Lupins
- Winter rainfall areas – March/April
- Summer rainfall areas – August/September

Sun hemp
- from October to January

The legumes can be turned in when the first flowers are fully open. Turn in the ryegrass when it is about 20 to 30 cm tall. Try and get all the material underground.

Horse manure: This is excellent for lightening heavy soils and can be used as an activator on the compost heap.

Liquid manure: Home-made liquid manure is quite useful as a tonic for plants and can be made as follows. Fill a sack with manure (any kind) and suspend it in a large drum of water. Move the sack up and down occasionally so that the water washes through the manure. The liquid will be ready to use after about a week. Dilute it until it is

Making a compost heap

There are compost bins on the market which are excellent for small gardens, but compost heaps are virtually essential in large gardens, where there is usually more material available and where more compost is needed.

If possible, site the compost heap where it is sheltered from wind and sun. The ideal ground size for a heap is 1,2 m x 3 m. Some gardeners prefer enclosing their heap/s with wire netting or wooden laths, others just mark the corners with four stout posts to help keep the material together. Enclosing the heap will keep it tidier, however, and a partition can also be made in the middle so that the material can be moved easily from one half to the other when it reaches the turning stage. The important point to remember is that the enclosure must allow for a free passage of air, as the micro-organisms need air to do their work of breaking down the material.

The ground under the heap should be firm. On this, place a 15 to 20 cm layer of vegetable matter and then sprinkle an activator on it. Animal manures, especially stable and poultry manure, are good activators. If these are not available then a commercial activator can be used, or ammonium sulphate at the rate of 15 g per square metre (i.e. 30 g for the size of the heap recommended). Add superphosphate at the rate of 10 g per square metre (15 g for this size heap). Also add wood ash if it is available. Water the layer lightly, pat down to exclude air pockets and cover with 5 cm of soil.

Repeat this 'sandwich', mixing soft and coarse vegetable matter as thoroughly as possible. This is especially important when using grass clippings. If left in a thick layer, air is excluded and the material does not break down but becomes a soggy mass. Coarse material, such as the stems of perennials and the stalks of cauliflowers and cabbages, should be chopped up before being put on the heap.

All vegetable waste can be composted, except: diseased plants; weeds which have gone to seed (in theory the heat of composting should destroy these, but this seldom happens); weeds with bulbous roots such as oxalis, onion weed and watergrass or uintjie; and prunings.

Cover the heap with soil when it is about 1,2 m high. The heap should be kept damp but not sodden. In dry weather it should be watered about once a week. During summer the material breaks down rapidly and in four to five weeks should be ready for turning. In winter it may take about six weeks. When turning compost ensure that the material that was on the outside of the heap ends up in the middle of the new heap. When the turning has been completed, cover the heap with soil again and leave until the compost is needed, when it should be dark and crumbly, with a pleasant, earthy smell.

Other organic fertilisers

Bone meal: This has also been used for many centuries as a fertiliser. It has a high phosphate content and this is released slowly. Apply 50 to 100 g per square metre, at any time of the year. It is not easily obtainable in this country.

Dried blood: This has a high nitrogen content. It is quick acting but also lasts over quite a long period. It is best applied as a liquid, mixed at the rate of 25 g of dried blood to 10 litres of water. It is not easily obtainable.

Guano: This is a fertiliser made from the droppings of sea birds and has a rough analysis of 2-12% N: 10-12% P: 2-3% K. This is a quick-acting fertiliser and is best applied at the rate of 50 to 100 g per square metre one or two weeks before planting. It has rather an unpleasant smell.

Mushroom compost (or spent mushroom compost): This is useful as a soil conditioner and mulch. Contrary to popular belief, it has some nutritive value, the analysis being 1,8-3,4% N: 0,25-0,39% P: 1-2%K. It is alkaline and should not be used on acid-loving plants.

Seaweed: This has been used for centuries and is one of the best organic fertilisers as it not only has the major elements in it but also all the trace elements, and it is an excellent soil conditioner. It is particularly useful for reconditioning old gardens where the soil has been worked out by constant cropping.

Unfortunately milled seaweed is expensive in this country. It should be applied at the rate of 100 to 225 g per square metre for annuals and vegetables, and 55 to 85 g per square metre for fruit trees, shrubs and lawns. Liquid seaweed and fish emulsion, on the other hand, are freely available and can be used as liquid manure or for foliar feeding.

Those living at the coast can collect their own seaweed. It should be hosed down to wash off the salt, then chopped up while still wet, as once it has been allowed to dry it is difficult to cut. It can be dug in immediately at the rate of 5 to 10 kg per square metre, or it can also be composted. The chopped seaweed will decompose more slowly in the soil than in the compost heap.

Wood ash: This is becoming a thing of the past in cities, with the introduction of smokeless zones where gardeners can no longer burn their prunings. It is a valuable source of potash and can contain from 4 to 15% potash as well as other nutrients. The ash must be stored under cover as the potash in it is soluble. As the lime content of wood ash may be high, sometimes as much as 40%, it should never be used for acid-loving plants.

Mulch

This is invaluable, especially where there is often a big difference between the day and night temperatures, and where the rainfall is comparatively low and erratic.

A mulch helps to regulate soil temperature, conserve moisture and suppress weeds. A wide range of materials including stones, plastic, sawdust, straw, ground-up mealie cobs, peat, grass clippings and compost can be used as a mulch. When undecayed materials such as grass clippings and sawdust are used as a mulch, the soil bacteria, in breaking down the material, use up nitrogen. Gardeners must compensate for this and apply extra nitrogen in the form of ammonium sulphate or LAN (limestone ammonium nitrate).

When watering beds which have been mulched, take care to ensure that the water is penetrating the mulch and getting to the soil beneath. Some materials such as grass clippings, sawdust and peat form an almost impervious thatch and just absorb the water.

Soil conditioners

Peat: This is an organic material formed from deposits of vegetation which has grown in heathland or bog. The water covering the plant material prevented micro-organisms from breaking it down. Peat has little nutritive value but can hold up to 16 times its own weight of water, making it an invaluable soil conditioner. Although it is acid (imported peat being more so than the local product), vast quantities would have to be applied to bring the pH of the soil down any appreciable degree. It is useful for adding to the soil when preparing holes for acid-loving plants, as they then have a fairly acid medium in which to start growing.

Perlite: This is another water-holding substance and is used for striking cuttings, and in potting soils.

Vermiculite: This is mica which has been expanded by heat. It has no food value but a great water-holding capacity. It is used in seed sowing mixtures and potting soils. It is alkaline.

Potting mixtures

John Innes No. 1 mixture

For seed sowing

2 parts loam (good garden soil) sifted through a 9 mm sieve and sterilised if possible
1 part imported peat (sifted and dampened), or compost
1 part clean coarse sand

To 1 plastic bucket of this mixture (the average plastic bucket holds 9 or 10 litres) add:
10 g superphosphate
5 g agricultural lime

Mix all the ingredients together thoroughly.

John Innes No. 2 mixture

For pricking out and for pot plants

7 parts loam (good garden soil) sifted through a 9 mm sieve
3 parts imported peat (sifted and dampened) or compost
2 parts clean coarse sand

To 1 plastic bucket (the average plastic bucket holds 9 or 10 litres) of this mixture add 30 g of 2:3:2 (22), and mix well.

For ferns

1 part good friable soil
1 part imported peat or well made compost
1 part clean coarse sand

For cuttings

Use any of these:
(a) Clean coarse sand
(b) 2 parts clean coarse sand and
1 part imported peat
(c) John Innes mixture:
1 part friable soil
2 parts imported peat
3 parts clean coarse sand

Pests and diseases

In a garden which is watered and weeded regularly, and if the plants are fed, staked and correctly pruned, there should seldom be serious problems with pests and diseases. Regular care is the best way of ensuring that your garden flourishes and if the month by month guidance given throughout this book is followed carefully, problems can be kept to a minimum. But even in the best tended garden, problems will occur from time to time and these will need specific treatment. The most common pests and diseases are discussed in this chapter, along with advice on their eradication or control.

Animal pests such as aphids, scale, caterpillars, worms, bugs and beetles can only be controlled with insecticides or pesticides and often a specific insecticide has to be used to control a specific insect. Diseases on the other hand are often caused by fungi, themselves members of the plant kingdom, and can only be controlled with fungicides. Here again specific fungicides must be used for specific fungal diseases.

There is an exception to this. The lime sulphur that is used in winter on deciduous fruit trees, vines and roses acts as both fungicide, killing off the spores of the fungi on the stems, and as an insecticide, killing various insects and their eggs.

The do's and don'ts of handling garden chemicals

Pesticides, insecticides and fungicides are poisonous, and highly dangerous if inhaled, or if they come into contact with your skin. Read instructions very carefully and always bear the following do's and don'ts in mind.

Do

- Do wear protective clothing: rubber gloves and a mask (and provide these for your gardener).
- Do change your clothes immediately if they become contaminated.
- Do train your gardener in the safe use of pesticides. Supervise the spraying yourself.
- Do make sure that no crop is harvested before the necessary safety period has passed.
- Do consult a doctor without delay if a case of suspected poisoning occurs. Give the name of the product, and its manufacturer.
- Do ensure that no streams, ponds or swimming pools are contaminated.
- Do spray only when necessary to control a pest or disease.
- Do read the instructions on the container and follow them carefully.

Don't

- Don't store pesticides within reach of children.
- Don't use pesticides for any purpose other than that prescribed on the label.
- Don't ever clear the blocked nozzle of spraying equipment by sucking or blowing.
- Don't use pesticides at a higher concentration than that recommended on the label.
- Don't store pesticides in cupboards where any kind of food is kept.
- Don't eat or smoke while using pesticides.
- Don't spray or dust in windy conditions as there is danger of contamination to humans, animals, water supplies, swimming pools or vegetable crops.
- Don't allow children or animals near when mixing and applying pesticides.
- Don't mix or store pesticides in cold drink bottles, even if they are labelled. Small children cannot read.

Pests

Amaryllis caterpillar (or lily tiger or lily borer): Attacks only members of the amaryllis family. The caterpillar has black and yellow dots on its back (hence the name lily tiger). The moth lays her eggs on the leaves at night and when these hatch after about a week the tiny caterpillars bore into the leaves and, if left unchecked, will bore right down into the bulb. These caterpillars can do untold damage in a few days, and so, as a precaution, plants should be inspected every day.

Control: Spray thoroughly with Karbaspray, directing the spray right down into the holes in the bulbs if necessary.

American bollworm: See **Bollworm**

Ants: Not popular in the garden because they loosen the soil round plants, often disturbing the roots. They encourage aphids by transporting their eggs from plant to plant, and they chase off many of the predators which help to control insects.

Control: They can be controlled with Dyant, or prevented from climbing up the stems and trunks of plants by painting these with Pelton Insect Trapping Glue. (Also see **Termites)**

Aphids (or aphis, greenfly or plant lice): Small sucking insects which may be green, grey, black or orange. They increase at an alarming rate in spring when the sap is flowing freely. Besides sucking the sap of plants, they are vectors or carriers of virus diseases and they cause one type of peach leaf curl. Plants which are healthy, well nourished and watered regularly are less likely to be attacked than those which are neglected.

Control: Spray with Malathion, or with a systemic insecticide such as Metasystox that is taken up into the sap of the plant. One application of the latter should be sufficient to clear the garden for some three to four weeks. Marinure liquid seaweed discourages aphids as it is thought they do not like the iodine in it. (Also see **Woolly aphids**)

Army worm: This worm feeds on grass and is particularly fond of kikuyu. There are usually 'invasions' when hundreds of worms appear. The worms are light green at first, gradually getting darker as they age. They have an inverted 'V' mark on the front of the head when fully grown.

Control: Spray with Karbaspray.

Astylus beetle (or spotted astylus beetle): Slender, about 15 mm long, and pale yellow with black spots. It feeds on the pollen of plants, the young kernels of mealies and sometimes on strawberries.

Control: Dust ornamental plants with Karbadust or 2% Lindane powder. Pick beetles off edible plants by hand.

Australian bug (or fluted scale): What the gardener sees is the white, fluted egg sac which, if squashed, will turn red from the larvae within. The insects spread rapidly if left unchecked.

142. *All aphids breed at an alarming rate.*

143. *Winged and wingless aphids sucking the sap of buds.*

144. *Australian bugs sucking the sap from twigs.*

Control: Spray with Malathion mixed with a mineral oil such as Alboleum or Curoleum added at a quarter of the strength recommended on the container. If there are only a few insects or egg sacs, one can paint the stems of affected plants with equal quantities of methylated spirits and water. Pure methylated spirits can also be used.

Bagrada bug: The adults are about 6 mm long, black with yellow and orange spots, and an orange cross on the back. These pests are found mainly on cauliflowers, cabbages, stocks and other plants belonging to the stock family, such as alyssum and arabis. They usually attack in spring and, if the infestation is bad, they can kill young plants.

Control: Spray with Karbaspray.

Barberton daisy fly: The fly lays her eggs in the buds, and the larvae feeding on the petals cause distorted blooms and missing petals.

Control: Spray with Metasystox, Rogor or Lebaycid, use a bait splashed onto the leaves (see page 108), or treat the soil with Aphicide Granules.

Blister beetle: See **CMR beetle**

Bollworm (or American bollworm): The caterpillars in various shades of green always have characteristic white lines along their sides. The moth lays her minute, creamy-white eggs singly and the tiny caterpillars hatch within two or three days. They burrow into the buds, flowers or fruit of the plants on which the eggs were laid. Rose buds, snapdragon flowers and the fruit of tomatoes are common victims. Roses which have been attacked look as though the petals have been pierced with a needle. Gardeners frequently find well-developed caterpillars in snapdragons and tomatoes.

145. *Astylus beetles feed on pollen.*

146. *Leaves infested with citrus psylla.*

Control: Spray with Karbaspray. If the eggs are on rose buds they can be rubbed off by hand.

Brown beetle: See **Cockchafer beetle**

Carnation fly: The flies, which look like small house flies, lay their eggs in the buds, and the larvae eat all the petals, leaving the calyx hollow.

Control: Spray with Malathion or use bait (see page 108). Splash the bait onto the buds with a fairly large paint brush or make a hole in the lid of a bottle and shake the bait over the plants.

Citrus psylla: This is the small insect which causes the bumps seen so often on citrus leaves. For many years it was thought that the insect did no damage beyond disfiguring the leaves, but in 1965 it was discovered that it was responsible for transmitting 'greening' disease from plant to plant. This disease seriously affects the health of the trees and 'greens' the fruit, resulting in it colouring incompletely.

The female lays her eggs, which are bright orange and large enough to be seen, on the edges of the leaves. One female can lay up to 100 eggs a day. When the nymphs hatch they move to the undersides of the leaves to feed, deforming them and causing the 'bumps'.

Control: Spray with an insecticide that is taken up into the sap of the tree (a systemic insecticide) such as Metasystox or Rogor, or use Dursban or Hysheen. Make particular note of how many days must elapse before it is safe to harvest the fruit. Also note that Rogor should not be used on certain plants (such as the rough lemon), so it is important to read the directions carefully before using.

CMR beetle (or blister beetle): Quite a large, yet slender beetle with yellow and black bands across the body. They feed on flowers during the day and are particularly fond of white roses.

Control: It is difficult to control beetles which eat flowers. If the infestation is bad the flowers can be dusted with Karbadust, but the best alternative is to catch the beetles by hand while they are feeding. As a protective measure wear rubber gloves, as the beetles secrete cantharidine, an irritant which causes blisters.

Cockchafer (or brown or rose beetle): A small brown beetle which feeds on the foliage of many plants, especially of roses, fuchsias and grape vines. They feed at night and are active from November until January.

The larvae of the beetles are the so-called 'white worms' found in the garden. These are greyish-white with brown heads and six well-developed legs, and are usually curled up like the letter 'C'. They should be destroyed when turned up in the soil.

Control: Put out traps at night, catch the beetles by hand, or spray late in the afternoon with Karbaspray. Traps are commercially available.

Codling moth: This moth, with a wingspan of about 19 mm, has a bronze spot on the tip of the front wings. The female lays her small white eggs on leaves and fruits. The eggs hatch after about ten days and the tiny caterpillars crawl into the fruit, entering through the small hollow at the calyx end. They feed on the fruit for five to six weeks before burrowing out. They then crawl down the stem and (if it is smooth) they may go down to the ground to pupate, otherwise they crawl into crevices in the bark. The pest attacks apples, pears, quinces and sometimes apricots.

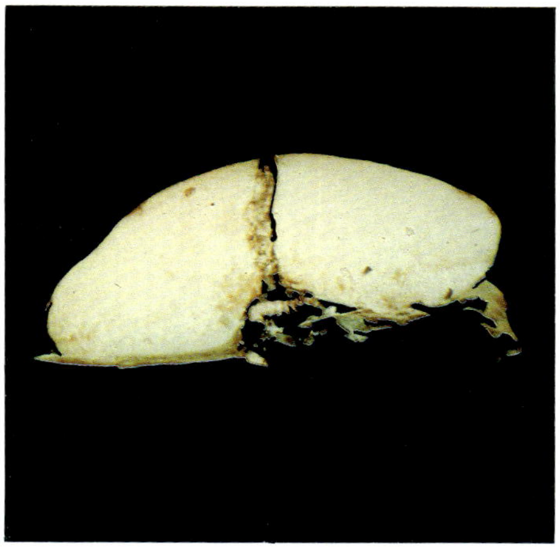

147. *Codling moth larva in an apple.*

Control: Spray the trees with Lebaycid or Ripcord, starting at three-quarter petal drop and repeating every four weeks and after heavy rain until 14 days before the fruit is to be harvested. The first application should be from above, as the calyx end of the small fruits is pointing upwards at that stage. Collect fallen fruit, soak it for a few hours in cold water to which a little paraffin has been added, then bury it. Alternatively, place the fallen fruit in a plastic refuse bag, tie the top of the bag tightly, and then dispose of it. Spray the trees thoroughly in winter with lime sulphur.

Lime sulphur

Lime sulphur may be used in winter on deciduous fruit trees, vines and rose bushes. It acts as both fungicide and insecticide. It kills off the spores of any fungi on the stems, and it kills various insects and their eggs.

'Winter strength' lime sulphur consists of 1 cup of lime sulphur mixed with 8 cups of water.

Never mix large quantities of lime sulphur at a time, as it oxidises quickly. Mix just enough to fill a spray can.

Never mix oil sprays with lime sulphur, as they are incompatible. Always wash and dry spraying equipment after use.

148. *Giant crickets may cause great damage to lawns.*

Fly baits

Baits are very useful for trapping fruit flies, gladiolus flies, carnation flies, Barberton daisy flies and pumpkin flies. Here are three baits that you can prepare yourself:

Malathion bait
Mix together:
18 ℓ water
1 kg white sugar
55 g 25% Malathion wettable powder
1 tablespoon brewer's yeast

Danex or Dipterex bait
Mix together:
10 ℓ water
800 g white sugar
5 g Danex or Dipterex
1 tablespoon brewer's yeast

Snykor Super or Snylok bait
Mix together:
18 ℓ water
1 kg white sugar
40 g Snykor Super or Snylok
1 tablespoon brewer's yeast

The brewer's yeast added to each of these baits apparently makes it even more attractive to the flies.

For fruit trees pour a little of the bait into a small jam jar or similar container and hang one container in each tree. Renew the bait once a week.

The bait can also be splashed onto large-leafed plants such as pumpkins, melons and squashes. Use an old whitewash brush or big paint brush and splash it on in large drops.

For smaller-leafed plants such as Barberton daisies, carnations and members of the cucumber family, put the bait into a bottle, pierce a hole in the lid and then shake the bait over the leaves.

Cricket: There are many species of true crickets in South Africa, the commonest being:
Garden cricket: These are dark coloured, small to medium-sized insects, with long antennae. They feed on seedlings both in trays and when they have been planted out into the garden. They are particularly fond of stocks, pansies and nicotianas.
Giant cricket: These are much larger and can reach a length of 7,5 cm. They have powerful jaws like pruning shears. Their holes, in sandy soils, can be about 60 cm deep, but in lawns the hole is usually about 30 cm deep. During the day these crickets hide in their holes and come out at night to feed. They are particularly fond of young tomato plants. On lawns they eat the grass round their holes causing it to die off in round patches.
Mole cricket: These are large russet-brown insects with front legs adapted for burrowing into the ground. They come out at night and will eat potatoes, roots and seedlings, especially those of marigolds.

Control: To control all of the above crickets pour Karbaspray or Dursban down the holes, or spray or dust the grass with any remedy which has gamma-BHC as the active ingredient.

Cut worm: The worms are dark grey to black and are found just below the surface of the soil. The moth lays her eggs on the leaves of plants, usually weeds. When the young caterpillars hatch they feed on these leaves for a few days before crawling down into the soil. They come out at night and eat through the stalks of young seedlings, making it seem that they have been cut off at ground level.

Control: Bait with Dipterex or Danex before planting out seedlings. If you notice that a seedling has been freshly cut off, the culprits can often be found by gently scratching round the stem, especially if it is in the early morning, or by pouring water round the stem and waiting for the worm to come up for air.

Eelworm: See **Nematodes**

Fluted scale: See **Australian bug**

Fruit beetle: Large, almost square beetles with black and yellow markings. They feed on fruit and flowers, especially peaches and rose blooms, preferring the pastel roses. They feed during the day and if disturbed fly off with a loud buzzing sound.

Control: Very difficult by spraying. The insects are best caught by hand. The grubs develop in compost, so it helps to keep the population down to some extent if one ensures that no decaying vegetation accumulates under hedges and in odd corners. Spraying with Karbaspray will help protect ornamentals.

Fruit fly: The flies, the size of large house flies, are brightly coloured and hold their wings out sideways. The female 'stings' the fruit with her sharp

149. *Fruit beetle feeding on a rose.*

ovipositor and lays her eggs just under the skin. Maggots hatch from the eggs after about two days and then eat their way down to the pip, causing the fruit to rot and fall off the tree. The maggots burrow their way out of the fallen fruit and into the ground, where they pupate. When the fly emerges about two weeks later, it is capable of burrowing through 50 to 60 cm of loose soil. It takes three weeks to mature and start its nefarious work again. The flies can live for six months. They feed on sweet liquids. During winter they live in evergreens and come out on warm, sunny days to feed.

Control: Rogor, Lebaycid or Ripcord can be used. When using Lebaycid start spraying the fruit when it is the size of a walnut and repeat every 10 days. Wet the trees thoroughly. The safety period is 10 days.

Bait during winter, spring and early summer (see page 108). Collect fallen fruit, soak it in water for a few hours to drown the maggots and then bury it. A little paraffin can also be added to the water in which the fruit is soaked to make doubly sure that the maggots are killed before being buried. Small amounts of fruit can be put in plastic bags which should be tightly tied, and then placed in the dustbin. It is important not to leave rotting fruit lying about in the garden as it provides an ideal environment for so many pests and diseases.

Ghost fly: See **White fly**

Gladiolus fly: This is a small fly which lays its eggs on the flower buds. The maggots burrow their way into the stem and feed on the pith, causing the buds to wither before they open.

Control: Dig or fork Aphicide Granulate into the soil around the plants when they are about 10 cm tall. Alternatively, spray the plants regularly every week with Karbaspray, using a spreader/sticker such as Spray-Stay to make it stick to the leaves, or use bait made of Malathion wettable powder or Danex (see page 108).

Lily borer: See **Amaryllis caterpillar**

Lily tiger: See **Amaryllis caterpillar**

Mealy bug: These attack a variety of plants: apple, apricot, guava and citrus trees, grape vines, green house plants and the base of leaves of agapanthus and similar plants. The insects are 6 to 8 mm in size and look like small tufts of cotton wool.

Control: Spray with Malathion mixed with a mineral oil such as Curoleum or Oleum, added at a quarter of the recommended strength. The insects are encouraged by ants which are attracted by the large amount of honeydew they secrete. The ants transport the eggs of the mealy bug to new plants, encouraging the spread of the pest. Ants must therefore be controlled as well.

Monkey beetle: This looks a little like the cockchafer beetle but has long, hairy back legs. Some are shiny brown, others metallic blue or green. They feed during the day, burrowing into the centre of flowers, especially marigolds and roses.

Control: Use Lindust, Bexadust or any other product containing gamma-BHC, or catch the beetles by hand. They breed in leaf mould in the veld and fly in to infest town gardens.

Nematodes (or eelworm): These are minute worms invisible to the naked eye. There are many types. Some invade roots while others invade leaves and stems. They all do serious damage.

Control: Nematodes are difficult to control. Crop rotation plays an important part in keeping the soil clean. Where leaf and stem nematodes are suspected, the plants can be sprayed with a systemic insecticide such as Metasystox. When the flowers have faded, the infected parts of the plant should be destroyed. Pull up annuals and cut down perennials. Fumigate the ground with chemicals such as Fumozone.

Pear slug (or slug worm): This black, slimy, slug-like creature, about 1 cm long, is the larva of the sawfly. The female sawfly cuts a slit in the underside of a leaf and glues her egg into this. When the larva hatches it bores its way to the upper surface where it feeds on the tissues, leaving only a skeleton of veins and mid-rib. It attacks pear, cherry, quince and plum trees, including the ornamental varieties. Badly infested trees lose all their leaves. The slug pupates in the soil.

Control: Wait until the fruit has been harvested and then spray with Karbaspray. Light cultivation of the soil under the trees during winter destroys many of the pupae.

Pernicious scale: See **Scale, Pernicious**

Potato ladybird: This insect is sometimes called the tortoise beetle because its shape and markings resemble those of a tortoise. While all other ladybirds are beneficial, this ladybird feeds on the leaves of certain plants. It prefers those of the potato plant, but also eats pumpkin, marrow, cucumber, turnip, radish, bean and spinach leaves.

Control: Use any remedy which has gamma-BHC as the active ingredient.

Pumpkin fly: There are several species, of which all are fairly large (about 19 mm long). They look rather like small wasps. They attack all members of the cucumber family (pumpkins, melons, and squashes). The female 'stings' the small fruits and deposits her eggs, and the maggots which develop from the eggs cause the fruit to rot.

Control: Use bait once a week and after heavy rain. Baits can be made with Malathion wettable powder, Danex, Dipterex, Snykor Super or Snylok (see page 108). Splash the bait onto the leaves using a white-wash brush or large paint brush, or make holes in the lid of a bottle and shake the bait over the leaves.

Red spider: A very small insect which is not really a spider but a mite. It gets its common name because it spins a fine silky web on the undersides of leaves.

Infected leaves have a yellow, stippled appearance and, if examined on the underside, the reddish mites, which look like grains of sand, can be seen crawling round. The insects thrive in hot, dry weather and multiply at a terrific rate. Although they attack a wide range of plants, they are particu-

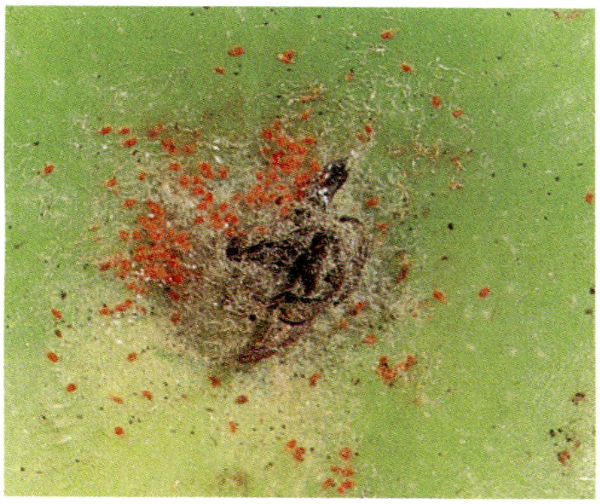

150. *Red spider mites thrive in hot dry weather.*

larly troublesome on those with hairy leaves such as Cape gooseberries, primroses, polyanthus, hollyhocks and foxgloves.

Control: Spray with Dursban, Dazzel, Metasystox, Rogor, Mitac or light/ medium mineral oil such as Alboleum, Curoleum, or Oleum, all of which can be purchased from a garden shop or nursery. Alternatively, dust with sulphur or Kelthane every fortnight until the infestation has cleared up. Keep plants well watered during dry weather. Hose down the foliage, especially the undersides of the leaves.

151. *Cockchafer beetle feeding on a rose.*

152. *Snails feed on foliage and flowers.*

Rose beetle: See **Cockchafer beetle**

Scale:

Pernicious scale: A serious pest to roses, apples, apricots, cherries, peaches, pears and plums. The scale is round, and black when small, changing to buff-grey when mature. They suck the sap of the plants and are toxic, being particularly poisonous to peach trees.

Control: Spray with two or three applications of 'winter strength' lime sulphur during winter, or with mineral oils such as Alboleum, Curoleum or Oleum. Never use lime sulphur and oil sprays together, as they are incompatible. If some scale is noticed on roses during summer it can be treated by painting the stems with a solution of equal quantities of methylated spirits and water.

Soft scale: These soft brown scales are found on ferns and other plants, usually along the mid-ribs of the leaves. The insects secrete honeydew and are encouraged by ants.

Control: Spray with Malathion or Karbaspray, using at half strength on ferns, or paint with equal quantities of methylated spirits and water. If the ants are controlled the scale usually disappears.

White scale: These are small, elongated, white scales which attack a number of plants, including aloes.

Control: Spray with Malathion mixed with a mineral oil such as Alboleum, Curoleum or Oleum at half the recommended strength, two or three times, at 10 day intervals.

Shield bug: See **Stink bug**

Slug: There are two types of slug. The smaller grey-black slug, about 15 mm long, is the more common. The larger yellow-brown slug is from 2 to 3 cm long. Slugs have a number of rasping 'teeth' and can do untold damage in the garden, especially to seedlings and other soft plants. They prefer moist conditions and are often found under stones and leaves. They are active throughout the year.

Control: Put out bait round plants in the evening, especially after rain or after watering the garden. There are a number of good proprietary baits available. A home-made bait consisting of 1 tablet of Meta solid fuel mixed with 2 cups of mealie meal is also effective. Crush the Meta finely, mix it well with the mealie meal and distribute this mixture in small heaps (of about a teaspoonful) around seedlings when the soil is damp. Slugs can also be trapped with half orange peels or cabbage leaves rubbed with dripping, placed on the ground. Inspect the traps each morning and collect up the slugs.

Slug worm: See **Pear slug**

Snail: Like slugs they too have numerous rasping 'teeth' and wreak havoc among beds of seedlings and other soft plants.

Snails must have lime to make their shells and will not be found where the soil is acid. During very dry weather they seal themselves against stones, bricks and walls. In the winter rainfall areas they are most active in winter, and in the summer rainfall areas they are most plentiful in summer.

Control: Put out bait in the evening, especially after rain and watering (use the same baits recommended for slugs). The population can be reduced considerably by catching the snails after rain or early in the morning when the plants are wet with dew.

Sodweb worm: This is quite a large worm which makes a hole in the lawn and covers this with a little trap door of web. The worms come out at night to feed on the grass, causing brown patches.

Control: Spray the grass with Karbaspray in the late afternoon. If damp sacks are left on the lawn at night a great many worms will be found under them in the morning and they can then be killed.

153. *The black stink bug sucks the sap of leaves and stems.*

Soft scale: See **Scale, Soft**

Stink bug (or shield bug): There are two types often found in the garden:

Black stink bug (or tip wilter): The large black bug is often called a 'tip wilter' as it pierces the tips of stems, causing them to wilt. It is particularly fond of dahlias.

Control: In the home garden the best way of dealing with this pest is to knock the insects off into a tin containing water and a little paraffin.

Green stink bug: This is about 13 mm long and a greyish-green colour. The insects attack vegetables such as beans and tomatoes, as well as peaches and pears, where they cause small distorted patches on the fruit.

Control: The same as for the black stink bugs. Spray peach trees with Karbaspray while the fruit is still green.

Termites (or white ants): There are two types of termites of interest to gardeners:

Harvester termite: These live on grass and non-woody plant material containing cellulose, and they infest lawns.

Wood destroying termite: These feed on wood and will attack the bark of trees and shrubs.

Control: To control both of the above termites scatter Karbadust round the holes when the termites are active. Repeat two to four days later and again after ten days if the activity has not stopped. Alternatively, pour 1 ℓ of Volaton into an active nest.

Thrip (or thrips): A small, delicate insect which sucks the sap of plants, leaving small marks on leaves or petals. Most gardeners are familiar with the white marks left on gladiolus flowers and pansy petals. Not only does the insect damage plants, but it is also a vector or carrier of virus diseases.

Control: Spray with Malathion, Metasystox, Rogor or Protex, or any insecticide which has gamma-BHC as the active ingredient. Alternatively, dust with sulphur.

Tip wilter: See **Stink bug, black**

White fly (or ghost fly): This is a tiny winged insect, about 3 mm long, covered with fine, waxy, white powder. After hatching, the insects settle down on the undersides of the leaves to feed. Badly infested leaves turn yellow, then dry up and fall off. There are several species, the most serious one from an economic point of view being that which attacks tobacco plants. This species also attacks tomato, pumpkin, bean and stoep plants, notably fuchsias. It is also a carrier of virus disease in tobacco.

Control: Spray with Sumicidin.

White scale: See **Scale, White**

Woolly aphids: These are small insects with white wax coverings which look like tufts of cotton wool. If held against the light the body fluids glow red. It is a serious pest on apple trees.

Control: Spray with a systemic insecticide such as Metasystox or Rogor which enters the sap of the plant. Allow at least three weeks to pass before harvesting the fruit.

Diseases

Black spot: A fungus which attacks roses, citrus and quinces. In roses black spots, each surrounded by a yellow ring, appear on the leaves, and if the disease is not checked plants may lose all their leaves.

Control: It is better to take preventive measures, as once the disease has appeared it is difficult to control. Start spraying rose bushes at the beginning of November, and spray regularly every seven to ten days and after heavy rain until the end of March or later in warm areas. Use Dithane, Mildane, Milrust, Antracol or Funginex. Pick off infected leaves and burn them. After pruning spray the bushes with 'winter strength' lime sulphur. Wait ten days and then spray again.

Blight:

Early blight: This fungus disease is particularly prevalent among potatoes and tomatoes, and it spreads rapidly. It appears as very dark brown, almost black, oval spots narrowly zoned with yellow tissue.

Follow a regular programme of spraying from the time tomatoes are still at the seedling stage and from the time potatoes first thrust their foliage above the ground. It is important to prevent the disease attacking, because once it has attacked no amount of spraying will save the crop. This disease is particularly prevalent during prolonged periods of overcast or wet weather but, even in the absence of these conditions, regular spraying should be routine.

Control: Spray every seven days with Antracol, copper-oxychloride or Dithane. If it rains re-spray as soon as the foliage dries.

Late blight: This disease may spread very rapidly among potatoes and tomatoes, particularly during wet weather. Leaves show spots of dead tissue and these rapidly enlarge, extending to the stems and showing a light, powdery growth. Tubers of infected potato plants may rot in the ground and the fruit of tomatoes turn brown, harden and decay.

Control: Spray as for early blight, every seven days during cloudy weather, and more frequently if the spray is washed off by rain. Spray every 12 days or so during settled, sunny weather.

Damping off: During hot, humid weather a fungus attacks seedlings at ground level, causing them to collapse. Sterilising the soil helps prevent the trouble, as does correct watering, which must be done early in the day so that the soil in the seed trays is not too wet at night. Well-drained soil is another help.

Control: Spray the trays with any one of the copper sprays, or with Dithane or Benlate.

Fungus: See **Lawn fungus**

Greening: See **Citrus psylla**

Lawn fungus: The following fungi all

attack lawn grass. As these fungi are difficult to control prevention is a better policy and the following measures will minimise the danger of the grass being infected: water in the morning; mow the grass regularly and keep it short; scarify and aerate well in spring; and feed the grass with a balanced fertiliser which contains potash.

Brown patch: Large circular patches develop and the grass has a bluish, water-soaked appearance with a smoky ring at the outer edges. These symptoms develop during hot, humid weather. Grass with soft, sappy growth as a result of being fed with a nitrogenous fertiliser is more susceptible than that which has been given a balanced fertiliser such as 2:3:2.

Control: Aerate affected areas and apply Dithane. As a preventive measure, in autumn soak the lawn with Bordeaux mixture, using 15 g per square metre.

Dollar spot: Small, circular, bleached patches about the size of a 50 cent piece develop under moist, humid conditions. If left unchecked the spots may spread and join and damage the grass seriously.

Control: Spray the infected areas thoroughly with Dithane and feed the grass with a nitrogenous fertiliser, for example, ammonium sulphate, at the rate of 15 g per square metre. Spray again after a fortnight.

Fairy ring: The grass dies off in distinctive rings. As the fungus decays and moves outwards the grass grows well because of the extra nitrogen it has received from the decayed material, and dark green rings show up.

Control: There is no satisfactory control for this disease. The best one can do is aerate the rings well to allow water to penetrate, and treat with Bordeaux mixture at the rate of 15 g per square metre.

Fusarium patch: Brown patches, some quite small, appear on the lawn and when the weather is humid the white or slightly pink cottony mycelium can be seen. This usually occurs in spring and autumn.

Control: Keep the grass short and aerate the infected patches. Each week apply a fungicide such as Dithane until the grass recovers.

Leaf curl (or peach leaf curl): Leaf curl caused by fungus usually occurs in wet weather, and affects peach and nectarine trees. The leaves develop large blisters which are often tinged pink.

Control: Spray the trees with a copper fungicide at bud swell. Spray very thoroughly twice again in winter with lime sulphur, allowing 10 days between applications.

Mildew:

Downy mildew: This is less common than **Powdery mildew,** but it can cause much damage, particularly to grapes, during wet weather which is favourable for its distribution. It first appears as downy white tufts on the underside of the leaves.

Control: When shoots are about 10 cm long, spray with Dithane, repeating this treatment at 10 day intervals. Copper-oxychloride may also be used.

Powdery mildew: There are a number of organisms which cause powdery mildew on vines, vegetables, roses and other plants. The disease attacks buds, leaves and stems and the powdery appearance is actually caused by felt-like masses of mycelium, which cover the surfaces of the plant. From this mycelium, upright growths arise at intervals and bear chains of spores at their free ends, giving a powdery look. These spores are carried by wind to other leaf surfaces where they germinate, so spreading the disease. Damage may be quite serious: leaves fall prematurely, buds fail to mature and fruit lesions develop.

Control: Fairly severe winter pruning helps. Burn all severed material and follow pruning immediately by spraying with lime sulphur. Wait 10 days and then spray again. When the plants are in early leaf administer a further two sprayings of Benlate, 15 days apart.

Peach leaf curl: See **Leaf curl**

Rust: There are many different rust fungi that attack garden plants including carnations, gladioli, fruit trees, roses and other flowering plants. Rust is more likely to occur in damp weather. Small rusty coloured spots appear on the leaves. Rust occurs on rose bushes at the coast but is not often seen on bushes inland.

Control: Spray regularly with Dithane, Plantvax or a copper spray, paying particular attention to the undersides of the leaves. Funginex can also be used. Use a spreader such as Spray-Stay to make the spray stick to the leaves.

Sooty mould: This is not actually a plant disease but a mould which forms on leaves when there is a honeydew secretion from aphids or other insects.

Control: Once the insect pest has been controlled, the mould will clear up. The leaves can be sprayed with soapy water (use Sunlight soap) to clean them.

Spots and blotches: These may be caused by fungi or bacteria.

Control: Those caused by fungi can be controlled by spraying with Dithane or a copper spray applied weekly until the trouble has cleared up. Those caused by bacterial infections are not easy to control but a copper spray or Dithane often helps.

Viruses: These attack many plants and may cause twisted or distorted leaves, or streaks, mottling or mosaic patterns on the foliage. Viruses can be transmitted to healthy plants by insects (such as aphids, white flies and thrips), by secateurs (when pruning or cutting flowers), or by the gardener's hands.

Control: There is no cure and infected plants should be pulled up and burnt.

Wilt: This can be caused by fungi or bacteria.

Control: They are all extremely difficult to control. Good drainage, crop rotation and garden hygiene can help to a certain extent.

The gardener's friends

Gardeners have many friends and allies in the insect world, and it is in the gardener's own interests to encourage and protect those insects which prey on garden pests. Choose insecticides which are least harmful to them, and do not spray indiscriminately but only when absolutely necessary.

Here is a list of the gardener's friends and how they help keep pests under control:

Birds: Many birds such as wagtails, white-eyes, swallows, swifts and shrikes (butcher birds) help the gardener by eating insect pests.

Hover flies: These are usually yellow and black, and can often be seen hovering over aphid-infested plants. They

lay their eggs among the aphids. The larvae which hatch from these eggs are legless and look like minute green torpedoes, and they devour aphids voraciously.

Lacewings: These are delicate little insects with transparent wings. Although there are a number of different kinds of lacewings perhaps the green and the brown are the most common. They feed on the larvae of mealy bugs, and on aphids.

Ladybirds (or ladybird beetles): There are a number of different species of this pretty beetle, and all except the potato ladybird are helpful to the gardener. The *Vedalia* ladybird feeds on the Australian bug (sometimes known as fluted scale) and has played a large part in controlling this pest on citrus. A small black species of ladybird feeds on the citrus mealy bug. The ant is the ladybird's enemy, so it pays to keep ants away. Some of the smaller ladybirds feed on scale, and they and their larvae feed voraciously on aphids.

Praying mantis (or Hottentot god): Many of these are green, but some are prettily coloured, or camouflaged to blend with their surroundings. The female lays her eggs in a whitish capsule which she glues to the stems of plants. Look out for this egg-case and do not destroy it. The young mantises start eating aphids as soon as they hatch. The adults eat aphids, flies, grasshoppers and other harmful insects.

Spiders: They depend on insects for their daily food, and so help control garden pests.

Wasps: These destroy many harmful insects. They do not eat their victims but either parasitise them (they lay their eggs in their victim's body so that when the young hatch they have food immediately available) or they paralyse their victims and leave them near their eggs in a prepared nest, again so that the young have food at hand when they hatch.

154. *A praying mantis, the gardener's ally.*
155. *Spiders help control many garden pests.*

Garden hygiene

Garden hygiene plays an important part in keeping plants healthy and free of pests. Rubbish which collects under hedges and in odd corners can harbour insects in winter. Shrubs and creepers which are allowed to become overgrown also provide a refuge for insects.

When annuals are past their best, pull them up and put them on the compost heap. Do the same with vegetables. Do not leave the stumps of cauliflowers and cabbages in the ground. Remove them and chop them up before putting them on the compost heap. If left in the ground they may harbour aphids and other insects.

Staking plants

Annuals and perennials which are not correctly staked also provide a refuge for insect pests. Stake bushy plants such as spray chrysanthemums. Place three or four stakes round the plants, then run two strands of stout string around the stakes.

The easiest way to stake plants such as stocks and tall marigolds is to place stakes at intervals on both sides of the rows and stretch stout string between them.

Weeds

Weeds not only harbour pests and diseases but they also rob plants of moisture and nutrients. Annual weeds seed profusely, often producing several generations a season. Never pass a weed in the garden: bend down and pull it up, and never let one go to seed. Remember the maxim: *'One year's seeding means seven years' weeding'*.

Perennial weeds are difficult to control once they have been allowed to get a foot, or rather, root hold. Most of them increase by vigorous vegetative methods and some produce seed as well. The most troublesome are:

Cyperus esculentus (yellow nutgrass, watergrass or uintjie) and **C. rotundus (red nutgrass, watergrass or uintjie):** These grasses increase by sending out rhizomes with small tubers (the uintjie) at the end, and also from seed. They are troublesome weeds in lawns and if eradication is done by hand ensure that the small 'uintjies' are removed. There is a specific weedkiller 'Ansar 529' for use on fine-leaved grasses. It is not suitable for coarse grasses such as kikuyu and Swazi. 'Ansar 529' is toxic and must be handled with great care. Drift and seepage will damage other plants in the vicinity.

Nothoscordium inodorum (onion weed or fragrant false garlic): Although the plant resembles garlic it does not have the same smell. The umbels of white flowers are fragrant and produce abundant seeds. The bulbs pull themselves deep down into the ground, often making it difficult to remove all the small bulbs which the mother plant produces. The only way to get rid of this persistent weed is to go over the ground again and again, removing small plants before they have time to pull themselves down and multiply. Remove the flower heads before they go to seed.

Oxalis latifolia (sorrel or red garden sorrel): The plants have scaly brown bulbs and from these they either send out runners with new bulbils at the end, or develop a fleshy tap root with numerous bulbils round the top. Although the plants produce pinky-mauve flowers, they do not seem to set seed. It needs patience and persistence to get rid of this weed as every little bulbil left in the ground starts a new colony.

Solanum mauritianum (bug tree): This grows into a large shrub or small tree. The large, furry leaves have an unpleasant smell when bruised. The flowers are mauve-blue and look like large potato flowers. These are followed by fairly large berries which turn yellow when ripe and are much loved by birds and fruit fly. The tree is a host plant for fruit fly. Although listed as a noxious weed for the whole of the Republic, it is none the less quite often seen.

Weedkillers

There are weedkillers for every type of weed, and gardeners should consult their nurseries if they need help in selecting the correct one. All weedkillers are toxic and must be handled with extreme care. Seepage and drift will damage plants in the vicinity. A container in which weedkiller has been mixed should never ever be used for any other purpose, for no matter how well the container has been washed there may still be a poisonous residue.

SUMMARY

Control of pests and diseases

Many of the substances listed below are extremely poisonous to humans, animals, birds, and other plants. Great care must be taken when using them. The number of days in brackets indicates the *safety period i.e. how many days to wait after using a fungicide or insecticide before it is safe to pick and eat that fruit or vegetable.*

Active ingredients	*Trade names*	*Pest/disease and plants affected*
Amitraz	Mitac, Red Spidersprey	Red spider – ornamentals
Benomyl	Benlate	Anthracnose – avocados (1 day) Black spot – citrus (14 days), roses Blossom blight – apricots, peaches, plums Botrytis rot – vines (14 days) Brown rot – peaches (7 days), tomatoes (3 days) Bulb and corm rot – ornamentals Freckle – peaches (7 days) Powdery mildew – apples (14 days), cucumber family (3 days), mangoes (30 days), pecans (3 days), roses, tomatoes (3 days) Ringspot – cabbage family (3 days) Scab – apples (14 days)
Bio-allethrin/piperonyl butoxide	Ant Insecticide	Ants (black and brown)
Bio-allethrin/pyrethrins/ piperonyl butoxide	Avi-Spray	Aphids
Bio-allethrin/phenothrin/ piperonyl butoxide/tetramethrin	Pyagra	General insecticide
Bromophos	Nexion, Protex	Ants (black and brown) Aphids – ornamentals Thrips – onion leaves (7 days), ornamentals
Bromophos/tetramethrin/ piperonyl butoxide	Nexion Plus	Ants (black and brown) Aphids – ornamentals Thrips – ornamentals
Butoxycarboxim	Plant Pin	Aphids and red spider – pot plants
Captab	Kaptan	Fungi – lawns

Active ingredients	*Trade names*	*Pest/disease and plants affected*
Carbaryl (compatible with most sprays)	Harakiri, Kamikaze, Karbadust, Karbaspray, Sevin	Amaryllis caterpillars – amaryllis family American bollworm – ornamentals Beetles of all types Bud mite – apples (7 days) Codling moth – apples and pears (7 days) Crickets – lawns Flower moth – aloes Flower pests – proteas Lawn caterpillars – lawns Leaf rollers – apples (7 days) Mealy bug – apples (7 days), vines (56 days) Stink bugs (shield bugs) – ornamentals Snout beetles – vines (56 days) Termites (white ants) – lawns
Carbaryl/gamma-BHC	Blue Death	Lawn caterpillars – lawns
Carbaryl/metaldehyde	Avisnail, Disa Snail Pellets, Protekta Snail Bait, Sevin Snail Bait, Slaklok, Sluggem, Slug and Snail Bait, Snail Ban, Snailfix, Snailflo, Snailjail, Snailsprey	Slugs and snails
Chlorpyrifos	Antsprey, Dursban, Hysheen, No Pest	American bollworm – citrus (10 days), tomatoes (4 days) Ants (black and brown) Aphids – peaches (30 days) Citrus psylla – citrus (60 days) Crickets – lawns Lawn caterpillars – lawns Mealy bug – apples, apricots, plums (spray in winter) Orange dog caterpillars – citrus (3 days) Pernicious scale – apples, apricots, peaches, plums (spray in winter), ornamentals Red spider – ornamentals Thrips – tomatoes (4 days) Wire worms – seed, newly germinated plants, roots of various crops
Copper oxychloride	Biltox, Copperchlor, Kopoxy, Cupravit, Virikop	Anthracnose – boysenberries (14 days), mangoes (14 days), vines (3 days) Bacterial blight – walnuts Bacterial canker – peaches (14 days) Bacterial spot – peaches (14 days) Black spot – citrus, plums (14 days), roses, tomatoes (3 days) Blossom end rot – guavas (14 days) Botrytis rot – vines (14 days) Dead arm – vines (14 days) Downy mildew – cabbage family (3 days), cucumber family (3 days), vines (3 days) Early blight – potatoes (14 days), tomatoes (3 days) Gum spot – apricots (14 days), peaches (14 days) Leaf curl – peaches (14 days)

Active ingredients	Trade names	Pest/disease and plants affected
		Leaf spot – celery (1 day), strawberries (14 days) Leaf and fruit spot – granadillas (3 days) Lumpy disease – guavas (14 days) Rust – carnations, gladioli, ornamentals Scab – apples (14 days), citrus, pecans
Copper oxychloride/ mercaptothion/sulphur	Orchard Dusting Powder, Rose and Garden, Rosegard	Aphids, fungi, red spider, thrips – combined pesticide and fungicide for orchards and roses
Copper oxychloride/ zineb	Miltox	Bacterial canker – peaches (14 days) Bacterial spot – cabbage family (3 days), mangoes (14 days), peaches (14 days), plums (14 days), tomatoes (3 days) Downy mildew – vines (14 days) Early blight – potatoes (14 days), tomatoes (3 days)
Copper sulphate/lime	Bordeaux mixture	General fungicide
Cyfluthrin	Baythroid H	General insecticide – ornamentals
Cyfluthrin/piperonyl butoxide	Baysol	Cockchafer beetles – roses Crickets – ornamentals Mealy bug – ornamentals Stink bugs (shield bugs) – ornamentals Thrips – ornamentals
Cypermethrin	Barricade, Cymbush, Ripcord	American bollworm – beans, tomatoes (7 days) Codling moth – apples and pears (14 days) Cutworms – seedlings False codling moth – peaches (14 days) Fruit fly – apples, peaches and pears (14 days)
Diazinon	Cremate, Dazzel, Direthrin, Extermadazz, Kayazinon	Aphids – beans (14 days), cabbage family (14 days), ornamentals, peaches (14 days), tomatoes (14 days)
Dichlorvos	Dyall, Lawn Caterpillar Killer	Aphids – cabbage family (2 days) Blotch leaf miner – proteas Diamond-back moth – cabbage family (2 days) Mealy bug – ornamentals, vines (7 days) Pear slug – cherries (2 days) Plusia looper – beans (3 days), tomatoes (2 days)
Dichlorvos/tetramethrin	Kilal	General insecticide
Dicofol	Kelthane	Red spider – beans (7 days), cherries (14 days), cabbage family (7 days), cucumber family (7 days), ornamentals, peaches (14 days), peas (7 days), peppers (7 days), quinces (14 days), tomatoes (7 days)

Active ingredients	*Trade names*	*Pest/disease and plants affected*
Dimethoate	Aphicide, Aphid Granulate, Aphikil, Pestox, Proteka A, Rogor, Insecticide Granules, Systemic Aphicide	Aphids – beans (14 days), citrus (14 days), cabbage family (14 days), cucumber family (14 days), ornamentals, peaches (28 days), strawberries (14 days) Black moth – proteas Bryobia mite – apples (14 days), peaches (28 days) Codling moth – apples and pears (14 days) Mealy bug – apples (14 days), vines (28 days) Red scale – ornamentals Red spider – ornamentals Woolly aphids – apples (14 days)
Dinocap	Karathane	Powdery mildew – cucumber family (14 days), grapes up to pea size, ornamentals, roses
Fenitrothion	Kontakil	Mealy bug – apples (spray in winter and at green tip stage)
Fenthion	Lebaycid	Bryobia mite – apples (10 days), apricots (10 days), pears (10 days) Codling moth – apples (10 days), pears (10 days), quinces (10 days) Fruit fly – stone fruits (10 days) Pumpkin fly – cucumber family (10 days)
Fenvalerate	Sumicidin	Flies (including white or ghost fly)
Formothion	Anthio, Medit	Fruit fly – stone fruits (10 days)
Gamma-BHC	Agronex, Ant, Ant and Garden Spray, Anticide, Bexadust, Dyant, Gamma-Ant, Lindaan, Lindan, Lindust	Ants (both black and brown) Aphids – beans (30 days), cabbage family (30 days), ornamentals Bagrada bug – cabbage family (30 days) CMR beetles – ornamentals Diamond-back moth – cabbage family (30 days) Eight-back bug – aloes Lawn caterpillars – lawns Potato ladybird – potatoes (30 days) Stink bugs (shield bugs) – ornamentals Small stink bug – ornamentals Snout beetles – aloes Thrips – beans (30 days), onion leaves (14 days) Wire worms – seed, newly germinated plants, roots of various crops
Mancozeb	Dithane	Anthracnose – cucumber family (3 days) Black spot – citrus, roses Blossom end rot – guavas (14 days) Brown rot – citrus (14 days) Downy mildew – boysenberries (14 days), cabbage family (3 days), cucumber family (except musk melons) (3 days), onions, ornamentals, peas (3 days), vines (14 days) Early blight – tomatoes (3 days) Leaf spot – ornamentals, chrysanthemums Freckle – peaches (28 days) Gum spot – apricots (14 days), peaches (28 days) Lumpy disease – guavas (14 days) Rust – apricots (28 days), beans (3 days), gladioli, peaches (28 days), plums (14 days) Rust mite – citrus (14 days) Scab – apples (spray at pre-blossom and green tip stage)

Active ingredients	*Trade names*	*Pest/disease and plants affected*
Mancozeb/sulphur	Milrust, Fungikill	Black spot – roses Downy mildew – onion leaves Early blight – potatoes (14 days), tomatoes (3 days)
Mercaptothion (not compatible with lime sulphur; lethal to aquatic animals)	Avigard, Beetle Spray, Bugdoom, Bulalazonke, Extermathion, Gardicide, Insekthion, Malasol, Malathion	Aphids – beans (7 days), ornamentals, peaches (14 days), pecan nuts (3 days) Australian bug – citrus (10 days) Bryobia mite – apples (10 days), peaches (10 days) CMR beetles – beans (7 days), ornamentals Diamond-back moth – cabbage family (7 days) Eight-back bug – aloes Lawn caterpillars – lawns Mealy bug – apples (10 days), granadillas (7 days), guavas (7 days), ornamentals, plums (10 days) Pear slug – apples, plums, cherries (spray after harvesting the fruit) Potato ladybird – cucumber family (1 day) Pumpkin fly – granadillas, cucumber family (use bait) Fruit fly – stone fruits (use bait) Red spider – ornamentals Scale: olive green scale – guavas (10 days); red scale – citrus (spray 6-8 weeks after petal drop); soft brown scale – ornamentals; soft scale – citrus (see red scale); white scale – aloes, granadillas (7 days) Woolly aphids – apples (10 days)
Mercaptothion/pyrethrins	Pythion	General insecticide – ornamentals
Metaldehyde	Disa Liquid Snail and Slug Killer, Flurosol, Metason, Snail Bait, Slugslak	Slugs and snails
Methiocarb	Mesurol	Slugs, snails and millipedes
Mineral oil light/medium (not compatible with lime sulphur)	Alboleum, Curoleum, Oleum	Australian bug – citrus Bryobia mite – apples Bud mite – apples Mealy bug – apples Pernicious scale – apples, ornamentals, peaches, plums, roses Red spider – ornamentals Scale: circular purple scale – citrus; mussle scale – citrus; red scale – citrus; soft brown scale – citrus, ornamentals; soft scale – granadillas; various scale – aloes
Oxydemeton-methyl	Metasystox R	Aphids – ornamentals, peaches (21 days) Bryobia mite – apples (21 days) Citrus psylla – citrus (21 days) Woolly aphids – apples (21 days)
Phoxim	Baythion, Volaton	Cutworms (use as bait)
Polysulphide sulphur (not compatible with mineral oils)	Lime sulphur	Fungi, insects, insect eggs – deciduous fruit trees, vines, roses (use as winter wash)

Active ingredients	*Trade names*	*Pest/disease and plants affected*
Primicarb	Pirimor	Aphids – ornamentals, peaches (21 days)
Propetamphos	Antkill	Ants (black and brown)
Propineb	Antracol	Anthracnose – vines (14 days) Black spot – roses Dead arm – vines (14 days) Early blight – potatoes (3 days), tomatoes (3 days) Downy mildew – boysenberries (14 days), vines (14 days)
Propineb/triadimefon	Bayleton 'A'	Black spot – roses
Pyrethrins/piperonyl butoxide	Insekil, Insekt, Pygarden	General insecticide – ornamentals
Sodium fluosilicate	Cutworm Bait, Harvester Termite Bait, Snylok, Snykor Super	Use as bait for cutworms, flies of all kinds, and termites (white and harvester ants)
Sulphur (dusting)	Thiovit	Erinose mite – Barberton daisies, peppers, vines Flat mite – citrus Grey mite – citrus Powdery mildew – mangoes, ornamentals, pawpaws, peaches, peas, peppers, roses, vines Red spider – beans, ornamentals, peppers Rust mite – citrus, tomatoes Rust – peaches, plums Silver mite – citrus Thrips – avocados, beans, citrus, ornamentals
Tetradifon	Redspidercide	Red spider – apples, peaches, pears, pot plants and many other plants
Thiometon	Ekatin	Aphids – beans (28 days), cabbage family (28 days), ornamentals, peaches (28 days), tomatoes (7 days)
Trichlorfon	Danex, Dipterex	Amaryllis caterpillar – amaryllis family Barberton daisy fly – Barberton daisies Carnation fly – carnations Diamond-back moth – cabbage family Plusia looper – tomatoes (3 days)
Triforine	Funginex, Fungisprey	Powdery mildew – cucumber family (1 day), ornamentals, roses Rust – beans (3 days), carnations, peas (3 days), roses

Glossary of terms

Amaryllis family: This includes clivias, crinums, day lilies, March lilies, nerines, and many others.
Annual: A plant that completes its life cycle (germinating, flowering, setting seed and then dying) all within a year. In South Africa annuals usually complete their cycle in one season.
Axil: The angle between a leaf or leaf stalk (petiole) and a stem.
Bare rooted (or ex open ground): Bare rooted plants, usually fruit trees, vines, berries and roses, are those that are dug up at the nursery and supplied without soil round their roots.
Broadleafed weeds: Where weedkillers are concerned a broadleafed weed is any weed other than grass.
Bud: An embryo shoot, flower or cluster of flowers.
Budding: A method of grafting widely used for the propagation of many plants, especially roses. (Also see **Stock.**)
Bulbs: These include true bulbs, corms, fleshy root stock, rhizomes, and stem tubers.
Cabbage family: This includes broccoli, Brussels sprouts, cabbages, cauliflowers, kale and kohlrabi.
Cold: Pig manure, for example, is 'cold'. It has a wetter, closer texture than horse or cow manure and does not heat up a compost heap as fast as they do.
Cucumber family: This includes cucumbers, melons (watermelons, sweet melons, spanspek), pumpkins and vegetable marrows (squashes).
Chlorosis: The lack of chlorophyll or green colouring matter in leaves as a result of which they become yellow or chlorotic.
Damping off: A general name given to various diseases which affect seedlings at or near soil level causing the stems to decay and the seedlings to topple over and die.
Defoliation: The shedding of leaves. It is natural for deciduous trees and shrubs to shed their leaves in autumn, but during the growing season defoliation may be caused by disease (e.g. black spot in roses), or by insects (e.g. a serious infestation of red spider), or by a deficiency of some nutrient (e.g. a lack of potassium in sweet peas).
Drip line (or drip circle): An imaginary circular line on the ground directly beneath the outer perimeter of the branches of a tree or shrub. Water tends to drip off the leaves onto this line.
Ex open ground: See **Bare rooted**
Eye: A term used in several different ways by gardeners. It may refer to the growth point of a tuber (e.g. the eye of a potato). The term may also refer to a growth bud in the axil of a leaf or leaf joint which may be cut off and used for propagation (e.g. the eye of a rose). (Also see **Budding.**)
General fungicide: A fungicide that will control most fungi.
General insecticide: An insecticide that will kill or control most insects.
Green tip stage: A bud is said to reach the green tip stage when the tips of the floral leaves within a bud begin to show.

Hardy: Hardy plants are those which can survive out of doors all year round without protection against frost. Hardy trees and shrubs are those which can withstand frost. Half hardy trees and shrubs are those which will withstand some frost if planted in a sheltered position, or, also in the case of trees, those which will survive frost once they have grown to above frost height (usually just over two metres in this country). Hardy summer annuals are those which will stand through winter as fairly small seedlings.
Heavy soil: The term generally applied to fine textured clay soils which retain moisture and drain slowly. Such soils are difficult to work when wet, and equally difficult to work when dry. They can be improved by the addition of humus and sand.
Heeling in: The process of planting temporarily until permanent planting can be done. A trench is dug in any convenient part of the garden and the plants are arranged in it with their roots close together. The soil is then replaced and firmed down over the roots. Plants heeled in can remain in good condition for some time.
Honeydew: The sticky sweet fluid secreted by aphids, scale and certain other insects. It is produced most abundantly in hot dry weather. It coats the surface of leaves, then goes mouldy producing a black mould which clogs the pores of the leaves. It is quite easy to wash off with a strong jet of water. Ants actually 'milk' aphids for their honeydew and encourage them by carrying them from plant to plant.
Humus: The residue left when any kind of organic matter decays. It is of immense importance in the soil as it improves soil texture, making it spongy and able to hold moisture without becoming waterlogged. Humus also provides a suitable medium for the beneficial bacteria that live in the soil. These bacteria feed on the many complex chemicals in the soil and in so doing break them down into suitable plant food. All humus is gradually destroyed by the natural process of decay and so more must be constantly added to keep the soil friable and fertile.
In situ: To sow in the open ground where the plants are to flower, rather than sowing in seed trays.

Lateral: A side shoot or branch, in contrast to a leading or terminal shoot found at the end of a branch.
Leaching: The removal of plant foods and other soluble matter from the soil by water draining through it. Plant foods leach out more readily from light sandy soils than from heavier soils.
Leaf mould: The dark powdery or flaky substance which results when leaves have been stacked and allowed to rot for sufficiently long. As a rule leaves stacked in autumn will be converted into good leaf mould by the following autumn. In good leaf mould the leaves break down into very small flakes, and one should not be able to find whole leaves or even recognisable fragments of leaves. Leaf mould is excellent in potting mixtures.
Leaf scar: The small scar left on the stem just below an eye or bud where a leaf has fallen off. The scar is often crescent shaped.
Mulch: A fairly heavy top dressing applied to the surface of the soil. Mulches feed the soil and the plants growing in it. Mulches also conserve moisture by slowing down surface evaporation, and they regulate soil temperature by providing insulation. Mulches can consist of fairly bulky organic matter such as strawy manure, compost or bark (obtainable from nurserymen). The looser the material the better it will conserve moisture and regulate soil temperature. Mulches can be applied at any time of the year.
Organic: Any chemical compound containing carbon. Many organic chemicals are derived from living animal or vegetable organisms and the term is often loosely used to describe substances obtained from such organisms, in contrast to those obtained from nonliving or artificial sources. For exam-

ple, organic gardening and organic manuring or organic fertilising make exclusive use of animal manures, vegetable composts, and fertilisers such as fish emulsion, seaweed meal, bone meal and dried blood.

Ornamental: An ornamental plant is grown purely for its appearance. It provides no food.

Peat: Organic matter in an arrested state of decay. Peat is formed from deposits of vegetation which has grown in heathland or bogs. It can absorb and hold up to sixteen times its own weight in water and is extremely useful as a soil conditioner. The best quality peat comes from Ireland, Great Britain, Canada and other northern countries.

Perennial: Any plant that continues to live for an indefinite number of years and which flowers year after year.

Pinching (or pinching back or stopping): The removal of the tips of growing shoots with the object of making the plant produce side shoots.

Pot bound: A plant is said to be pot bound when the roots fill the entire pot and the soil is exhausted. This happens especially when the plant has been growing in the same pot for a while.

Pot on (or repot): To remove a plant from its present pot and replant it in a larger pot (usually one size larger).

Pot up: To transfer a seedling or young plant from a seed tray to a plant pot.

Pricking out: The transference of seedlings from seed trays or pans to other receptacles where they can be given more space.

Root run: The area of soil occupied by the roots of a plant.

Scion: A cutting or bud of a desired plant which is grafted on to another plant which provides the root system. (Also see **Stock**.)

Standard: A standard is any tree or shrub grown on a bare stem several metres high. Standard roses are produced by allowing a briar stem to reach a required height and then inserting buds of the chosen variety at that level.

Stock (or root stock): The plant that provides the roots onto which the scion is grafted.

Stone fruits: These are fruits belonging to the prunus family i.e. apricots, cherries, nectarines, peaches and plums.

Stopping: See **Pinching**

Strike: Plants strike or produce a root or roots. To strike a cutting means to root a cutting.

Tender: A tender plant is one that would be injured by frost.

Thinning out: The process of reducing the number of plants growing in one place so that those which remain can have more space to develop, or reducing the number of shoots on any one plant, or reducing the number of flowers or fruits the plant produces. Crowded seedlings should be thinned out. If some of the flowers or small fruits on fruit trees are thinned out, the size and quality of the remaining fruit will be greatly improved.

Top dressing (or dressing): The application of soil, fertiliser, compost, lime or similar material to the surface of lawns or beds. A heavy top dressing of manure, compost etc. is usually referred to as a mulch.

Winter wash: An insecticide or fungicide that is applied to plants, specially fruit trees, during winter when plants are dormant.

General and plant index

This index includes subjects and plants described in this book. The common names of plants are cross referenced to the botanical names, where these have been used. Page numbers in **bold** refer to illustrations.